A TASTE OF
MOROCCO

NOTES FOR READERS

Bracketed terms are intended for American readers.

Standard level spoon measurements are used in all recipes:
1 tablespoon = one 15 ml spoon
1 teaspoon = one 5 ml spoon

The Moroccan pastry dough speciality of brik is mentioned in a number of recipes but, except for stores specializing in North African and Middle Eastern produce, it is not readily available in the UK and USA. The alternative of filo pastry is given, which will achieve the desired effect. Please follow the manufacturer's instructions carefully with regard to the handling of filo, as it dries out very easily.

Eggs should be medium (large) unless otherwise stated.

Milk should be full fat (whole) unless otherwise stated.

Pepper should be freshly ground unless otherwise stated.

Fresh herbs should be used unless otherwise stated and well rinsed. If unavailable use dried herbs as an alternative but halve the given quantity.

Ovens should be preheated to the specified temperature – if using a fan-assisted oven follow the manufacturer's instructions for adjusting the time and temperature.

Chicken and other poultry should be cooked thoroughly before serving. To test for this, deeply pierce the plumpest part of the bird with a sharp skewer or the point of a knife. If the juices run clear the chicken is ready.

This book contains dishes made from nuts and nut derivatives. It is advisable for readers with known allergic reactions to nuts and nut derivatives and those who may be potentially vulnerable to these allergies, such as pregnant and nursing mothers, invalids, the elderly, babies and children, to avoid dishes made with nuts and nut oils. It is also prudent to check the labels of ingredients for the possible inclusion of nut derivatives.

A TASTE OF
MOROCCO

Hervé Amiard / Laurence Mouton
Maria Seguin-Tsouli / Marie-Pascale Rauzier

CONTENTS الفهرس

Imperial City of Fès 19

Recipes

Cuisine and Culture

Coastal Regions of Morocco 85

Recipes

Cuisine and Culture

Marrakech and the South 127

Recipes

Cuisine and Culture

GASTRONOMIC MELTING POT

Moroccan cuisine draws its richness from the kingdom's turbulent history and from its ancient traditions. The different peoples who have traded with Morocco over the centuries, as well as those who invaded the country, have left traces of their passage not only in art and architecture but also in gastronomy.

From the original Berber population to the arrival of the Arabs, followed by the Andalusians and Jews who were expelled from Spain, and later Ottoman influences, Morocco's ethnic diversity and what it borrowed and imported from different continents have all contributed to the shaping of a cuisine that is famous, worldwide. To Morocco, cooking is a tradition, an expression of a culture and a civilization, the art of living and hospitality. In every home, tea and the accompanying array of cakes await the visitor, together with those symbols of hospitality, milk and dates.

From their Berber ancestors, Moroccans have inherited simple rustic dishes based on ground wheat, semolina, aromatic plants and spices. Arabs arrived from the East in the seventh century, conquering the whole of North Africa. They settled in Fès at the beginning of the ninth century and brought with them the refinements of Baghdad's sophisticated civilization. A masterpiece of culinary literature, *Kitab el Tabih*, written in 1226 by Chamseddine el Baghdadi, a gourmet from Baghdad, circulated in Cairo, Tunis, Algiers and Fès. Arab cuisine introduced to Morocco a new way of cooking meat and poultry, in sauce reduced at the end of the cooking process and flavoured with exotic spices such as saffron, nutmeg and ginger. The

Ommeyades from Syria passed on cake recipes based on flour, oil, honey, almonds and pistachios. However, the strongest influence on Moroccan cuisine, beyond a shadow of a doubt, has to be that of Andalusia. In the fifteenth century, after eight centuries of occupation, the Andalusian Arabs were driven out of the Iberian peninsula by the *Reconquista* (the Christian re-conquest of Spain). Granada, the last bastion of Spanish Islam, fell in that fateful year of 1492. Refugees settled in Tétouan, Fès and Rabat. They introduced a sophisticated way of life to these urban centres and, at the same time, brought with them their culinary traditions, a mixture of Jewish, Christian and Arab cuisines. All kinds of meat, fish and vegetables were included in their recipes, which were enhanced by selected spices. Sweet and savoury, mild and bitter were combined in one dish. The famous prune tagine, pigeon pastilla, grated onion mixture, parsley, ground almonds and cinnamon, lemon and olive tagine, stuffed meat and vegetables are all recipes that came from Andalusia or were adopted by the Andalusians. Borrowings from Ottoman, African and Western culture have been added to these Eastern and Spanish influences. A large number of Algerian families – whose country was occupied by the Turks from the beginning of the sixteenth century until 1830 – fled when the French occupied Algeria and then settled in Tétouan. Their cuisine, steeped in Turkish influences, spread to Moroccan brochettes and grills (broils), close relatives of Turkish kebabs, as well as sheets of fried pastry such as briouats.

ABOVE
With the last rays of the setting sun, a large open air 'restaurant' descends upon the Jemaa el Fnaa square, in Marrakech. Liver kebabs, steamed sheep's heads, bowls of harira or fried aubergines (eggplant) feed the diners till late into the night.

Undoubtedly, African influences go back a long way; there is also no doubt that trans-Saharan caravans have travelled the roads of Morocco from Sudan, for many a century, carrying with them new spices, vegetables and exotic fruits. As for English traders, they introduced tea to Morocco with a little more success than the French managed with the baguette and steak and chips. The great classics of Moroccan cuisine, like pastilla, couscous and tagines, are found throughout Morocco, from north to south, from east to west. Only the methods of preparation and ingredients vary from one region to another. Marrakech cuisine, with its *tangias* and spiced tagines, differs from the cuisine of Fès. The Saharans eat barley semolina couscous and are not familiar with seafood, while the coastal areas enjoy couscous made with cornmeal and fish. But as a result of the rural exodus, the differences become blurred, but family cooking traditions remain and endure.

WOMEN'S CUISINE

Pride in oral traditions, automatically handed down from mother to daughter, expert inimitable sleights of hand, Moroccan cuisine is the preserve of women, the supreme guardians of ancestral know-how. Their informed eye knows how to choose vegetables and meat with care, their nose orders the perfect measure of spices, their hands know instinctively the correct density of dough, the quality of a grain. Sight and touch more than compensate for the lack of precise measurement. For a long time, a girl couldn't consider getting married without knowing how to roll couscous grain between her fingers lovingly in order to prepare a fragrant tagine. In the countryside, illiterate women and girls are commonplace, but

they cook perfectly, from the knowledge passed down through generations of women in their families. Too often young girls are still 'exempted' from school — the female illiteracy rate still remains very high in Morocco — consequently they have plenty of time to watch and learn from the cooks at home. Women dedicate a large part of their day to preparing meals. This is their preserve. Meticulous and complex culinary preparation is all a matter of time. Women manage their ingredients and prepare those daily dishes for which they alone hold the secrets. The family gathers round the mother, the mistress of the kitchen, for meals. On special occasions, all the women, both family and friends, get together to help each other out. Excluded from the kitchen, it's the man, on the other hand, who is in charge outside. He tends the barbecue, turns the kebabs, and makes the mint tea. In today's urban world more and more Moroccan women work outside the home and their time is precious. In addition, recipes that take a long time to prepare are reserved for special occasions or just simplified. Cookery has been modernized, but the refrigerator, freezer, gas stove and food processor don't prevent cooks from remaining faithful to tradition, working with their hands, but gaining a little extra time from having all the mod cons.

Harking back to a time in the not so distant past, women still like to prepare conserves such as lemons macerated in salt, olives, or preserved meat...

THE RICHES OF VEGETABLE
GARDENS AND ORCHARDS

In general, an ordinary meal consists of a single dish and lots of bread. In the

FACING PAGE
Founts of ancestral knowledge, Moroccan cooks reign supreme in their own kitchens.

ABOVE
Few women possess the inimitable and essential dexterity to make trid, *large stretched out, oiled, transparent sheets of pastry that are stuffed with meat or poultry.*

country, it often consists of just simple thick soup. On the other hand, on festive occasions, copious dishes follow one another in a specific order. Numerous salads, are followed by pastilla, before the arrival of a stream of tagines and the final traditional couscous course.

Carrots, grated raw, served with orange juice and a dusting of cinnamon; green salads with orange; radish salads; onion salads; tomatoes and cucumbers; also carrots cooked with cumin, *zaalouk*; aubergine (eggplant) purée; charcoal-grilled (broiled) (bell) peppers cut in thin strips; vegetable fritters; these raw *hors d'oeuvres* and cooked vegetable purées, are all laid out on the table as multi-coloured appetizers, and are bound to whet your appetite. Often served as an accompaniment to meat or a couscous, vegetables can also be eaten as a main course. The flavour of the dish depends largely on the freshness of the vegetables. Their diversity and availability all the year round in the markets makes them one of the trump cards of Moroccan cuisine. In addition, the mistress of the house makes her choice in the souks with an almost fanatical care. Carrots, turnips, courgettes (zucchini), small and firm, aubergines (eggplant) with green stalks, are commonly used ingredients. Tomatoes have only been grown in Morocco since the beginning of the twentieth century, the time of the French protectorate, but today they are indispensable in Moroccan kitchens. In tagines and salads, tomatoes are always peeled and deseeded. Harvested from February onwards, broad (fava) beans are seasonal vegetables, as are artichokes and green asparagus, each in its own way, varying the flavour of tagines. Onions must be firm and big enough. Chickpeas (garbanzos) are soaked in water for

several hours before being peeled. Each vegetable has its own cooking time, which has to be respected to preserve its natural flavour.

Filled with sunshine, fruits complete a meal with a touch of freshness. Served fresh or as fruit salad, they are rich in sugar and vitamins and blend equally well with meat and vegetables, in numerous tagines. Oranges, grapefruit and lemons grow in abundance in the open country around Sous. The small bananas from the Agadir region are particularly sweet, honeydew melons and marbled watermelons provide refreshment on summer evenings, medlars have slightly acidic flesh and huge stones (pits). Small apricots are very fragrant and prickly pears are irresistible. Quinces are November fruits and often used as a vegetable accompaniment because of their slightly acid taste and sweetness.

MELT-IN-THE-MOUTH MEAT
AND CHOICE SPICES

Once a luxury foodstuff, mutton and lamb are the most commonly eaten meats. In couscous, shoulder, neck and leg of lamb are preferred.

These meats have a special place in religious festivals and celebrations (Aïd el Kebir, naming a newly-born,…). According to Muslim belief, animals must have their throats ritually slit while the name of Allah is invoked, for a meat to be *halal* or lawful. The eating of pork, or other animals that have not been consecrated prior to slaughter, is forbidden by Islam. When a sheep is sacrificed, every part of it is used. The meat is dried in the sun and keeps very well and is useful when preparing improvised meals for unexpected guests, provided it is well cooked.

ABOVE
Small hors d'oeuvres dishes, shaped like tagines, containing pepper and salt and sometimes cumin, decorate tables at every meal.

FACING PAGE
Vegetable souk in Fès.

Meat is only eaten cooked and well cooked at that. In the absence of cutlery, it has to be removed from the bone using only the fingers of the right hand. Eating beef is a recent development and eating veal is rare. Although chicken has long been considered a luxury dish, it nevertheless plays an important part in the Moroccan diet. Free-range chicken, raised in the open air, is appreciated for its firm flesh, with no risk of its disintegrating during cooking. As for organically reared chicken, it is cooked very quickly and doesn't have to be simmered. Chicken is always cleaned before being prepared and the neck, gizzard and liver are retained, to add flavour to the bouillon for couscous. Some recipes involve boiling for several hours, but meat is just as tasty, simply grilled (broiled) as kebabs dipped in cumin and cooked over charcoal or a wood fire, or on festive occasions on a spit over a fire. It needs to be cooked slowly and basted frequently so that it can easily be picked off the bone.

Without spices, seasoning, or fresh herbs, the cuisine would be bland and flavourless. Thanks to spices the range of dishes offers huge diversity, despite the fact that the number of base ingredients is limited. Spices are sold both loose and in bulk in the souks. Wise cooks buy these spices in small quantities and store them out of direct light in airtight jars, because once they are exposed to the air, the spices soon become stale and lose their flavour. Cinnamon sticks, root ginger, cloves, nutmeg… whole spices are preferable. Once grated, they exude mellow flavours. Commercially available pre-packed spice mixes are best avoided because they lose their individual pungency in blend format. The subtlety of

the perfect blend depends upon the art of mixing the exact proportions to create a balanced blend, without losing the flavour of the individual spices — this is work for an expert. Cumin and paprika or cinnamon and ginger are straightforward to blend. Certain spices are better at permeating meat and vegetables, at the start of the cooking process, whereas other spices, such as cumin, cinnamon or nutmeg are more appropriate for adding when cooking is complete, so as to avoid masking the flavours of the other spices.

Derived from the original round earthenware dish with its pointed lid, the term 'tagine' is now used, more commonly, to describe the actual contents. The heavy, earthenware construction of the tagine vessel protects food from open flames, while also making sure that the heat is evenly distributed; it is also ideal for slow simmering and braising. If large quantities of ingredients are involved, tagine dishes are usually cooked in a large cooking pot first and then transferred to a tagine dish for serving. Decorated with glazed motifs, the tagine dish adds a decorative feature at table, while its conical shaped lid also keeps the food warm. There are a hundred and one ways to prepare a tagine: based on meat, chicken, or fish, depending on regional availability; cooked in olive oil or groundnut (peanut) oil, accompanied by olives, prunes, raisins, lemons and quinces. The unique flavour of the finished dish is determined by the proportions and blend of spices used to cook the tagine. A perfect tagine is never greasy. The

sauces that coat the meat should be thick and smooth, but never runny. Tagine sauces are prepared in one of four different ways: *m'charmel* is a red sauce based on saffron, pepper, cumin, ginger and red chilli. *M'hamer* sauce is based on paprika, cumin and olive oil and, like *m'charmel*, lends a reddish colour to the tagine. *M'qualli* sauce, with saffron and ginger has a more yellowish colour, similar to *qadra* sauce which consists of thinly chopped onions, saffron, white pepper, ginger and butter. A little imagination, coupled with a great deal of skill completes the essential requirements for making a tagine. Coriander (cilantro), parsley, lemon, garlic, olives or honey are added, according to the recipes' base meat or vegetable ingredients. These sauces give their names to the dishes: tagine m'charmel, m'hamer chicken, etc. Fish tagines are always prepared or stuffed with *chermoula*, a garlic, coriander (cilantro), lemon, olive oil, paprika, cumin and parsley based marinade.

On middle-class, as well as more basic dining tables, couscous is a highly sociable dish, a dish served on Friday, after worship, a dish for festive occasions or ceremonies, for births, marriages and burials. Arranged on a round dish, it looks like a smooth-surfaced cone, soaked in a little bouillon sauce, while the meat and vegetables are arranged decoratively in the central cavity.

Enjoyed and highly-rated as a unique dish, couscous no longer retains its exclusivity, strictly speaking, because it is served as a final course at most *diffas* (banquets serving couscous). Simply consuming a few mouthfuls is considered sufficient to please the host. Made from wheat, barley or cornmeal and accompanied by vegetables and meat, couscous is always prepared in the same way. Although it is

ABOVE
Dried vegetables, spices, dried mint, roots or medicinal herbs are always sold loose, in large jute or plastic sacks.

rare, nowadays, for cooks to *roll* the semolina grains in a little flour and water, using the palms of their hands, genuine couscous is, nevertheless, made from swollen grains that are steamed, perfectly separated, light and lump-free. Above all, couscous requires quality grains. Even couscous that is bought 'ready for cooking' involves an elaborate three-stage procedure of steaming, cooling and mixing the grains with butter using the fingertips. Every region has its own specialities, every family its own preferences, every season its vegetables. Over the years, numerous local variations have been added, around the couscous base, which is typically accompanied by indigenous vegetables – carrots, onions, turnips. Couscous with seven vegetables is served in Casablanca – the number seven is considered to be a sign of good luck – but many other variations exist, depending on the region: cornmeal couscous in the Atlas, fish couscous in the coastal regions, meatball couscous, alfalfa couscous, mussel couscous, fig couscous, raisin couscous, with spices and almonds... Couscous grains are prepared and worked in a *gsââ* a large, round vessel made of wood or glazed earthenware. The metal couscoussier has largely replaced the rustic clay couscoussier, used in the past.

As with blending spices, knowing how to achieve precisely the correct mix of couscous is essential. Serving couscous with several different types of meat is a Western invention. Using just one kind of meat draws out more flavour from the vegetables and the bouillon. In addition to savoury couscous, sweetened versions exist, such as *seffa* – grains prepared with butter, sugar, cinnamon and honey.

In Morocco, the pleasures of eating are inextricably associated with the pleasures of entertaining guests. A nation of food lovers, the Moroccan people seize thousands of opportunities for family gatherings with parents, friends or strangers. Every festival is celebrated – religious, as well as numerous family occasions for rejoicing. In traditional houses, living rooms lined with benches covered in simple cretonne, velvet or rich brocade, stretch out lengthways, from large, white, blue and green, mosaic-tiled patios. These banquettes with their neatly arranged, well-padded cushions in the same fabric provide comfortable seating. Rabat carpets warm the tiled floors and give the living room a feeling of warmth and insulation. This layout with no sofas against the walls allows a large number of guests to be entertained at the same time. At mealtime, one or more round tables are shifted to a corner of the room. Being invited for a meal involves being warmly welcomed on arrival by the master of the house. Greeting etiquette, which merely requires a ritual response, is an obligatory token of politeness. Enquiries are made about the health of everyone, particularly children, amid expressions of mutual admiration. Entering someone's house to share a meal means putting time on hold and closing the door on the troubles of the outside world. The rules governing hospitality are a sacred duty. The serenity and gentleness of the mistress of the house belie a long and hard day's work in the kitchen, preparing a lavish meal involving numerous trips to and from the living room to check that nothing is missing. When the guests arrive, every-

ABOVE
Women organize the household provisions and visit the souks to hand pick the freshest vegetables, and to smell and taste the finest spices.

thing is ready. The atmosphere is fragrant with orange blossom. A burner releases the aroma of sandalwood. Water is boiling in the urn, for the tea. White embroidered tablecloths cover the round tables. Fès and Tétouan embroidery has motifs that recall the cross of Toledo. In Rabat and Salé, table linen is embroidered in scalloped blanket stitch, in pastel shades; Meknés is typified by its multicoloured embroidery, Azzemour by its needlepoint – each town boasts its own technique.

Once the guests have been seated at table, supported by the cushions on the banquettes, or seated on pouffes, the ritual common to all meals, and a skill that is acquired in early childhood, commences. A washstand ewer with a long spout is passed around the table. Rinsing one's hands is a fundamental part of the ritual. Likewise, the meal does not begin until the host has uttered the sacred word: *Bismillah.* Small side plates are placed in front of each guest, to be used for bread or small pieces of meat or bones. Salads, in small bowls or plates are arranged in a circle on the table, where they remain throughout, as an integral part of the meal. A feast for the eyes, place settings are laid out with consummate skill and the colour of the spices, olives and preserved lemons further enhance the enchanting scene. The meal offers generous portions in keeping with the host's generosity. A house that receives a few extra surprise guests never runs short of provisions. Meals are planned to cater for twice as many guests. Similarly, rushing through the various courses or leaving food on the plate is deemed an insult to the master of the house and very bad form indeed. Besides, such conduct also shows a disregard for the fact that the hosts

have to feed the rest of the household, including children and servants. In the centre of the table, the dishes are revealed, one by one, and in a specific sequence; diners are expected to savour each mouthful delicately and always eat in moderation. A pastilla, grilled (broiled) meat, a fish or chicken tagine … all are eaten from a common dish, using three fingers, the thumb, index finger and the third finger of the right hand, without getting in the way of the person sitting closest. Bread, of which there are always copious supplies, is used as a table utensil instead of cutlery because iron metal has always been considered unlucky throughout Muslim societies. Only spoons are allowed for eating the final course of couscous, which is accompanied by a large bowl of fruit, or sweet semolina, flavoured with cinnamon. Drinks, arranged on separate trays, are served on demand or at the end of the meal. Once the *Hamdullilah* has been pronounced by the master of the house, the guests may then withdraw from the table, to be ushered into another corner of the room, where large trays bearing tea and numerous small cakes await them.

FEASTS FOR SPECIAL OCCASIONS

Every significant stage in life is marked by festivities, family feasts and by culinary preparation. Religious festivals or family celebrations, the return from Mecca, the evenings of the month of Ramadan, all are a pretext for celebrating and enjoying special dishes associated with specific events.
Paradoxically, throughout the month of Ramadan, when Muslims are expected to fast throughout the day, food consumption increases dramatically. This is

the month when cooks spend most of their time preparing to eat, while fasting themselves. The main food item affected by this increase in consumption is the tomato. It is an essential ingredient in the preparation of *harira*, a thick, highly seasoned, tomato-based lemon-flavoured soup made with lentils, chickpeas (garbanzos), rice and meat, served in the evenings. Muslims fast from daybreak to sunset, renouncing all food and drink and the pleasures of the flesh, during the daytime. Before daybreak, the 'last meal', or *shor* consists of milk, sweetened semolina and pancakes. At sunset, *ftour* marks the end of the day's fast, and is announced by the sound of sirens in all towns and villages. For 30 days, steaming *harira* presides over all domestic dining tables. This substantial dish is accompanied by hard-boiled (hard-cooked) eggs, *sellou*, a mixture of toasted ground almonds and flour, sugar, cinnamon and butter; *chebbakiyas*, rich, succulent and aromatic honey cakes, dates, pancakes, coffee and milk.

Next, comes the tea, accompanied by the obligatory small cakes. In many families, dinner is served around midnight. The 26th day of Ramadan, known as *The Night of Destiny*, celebrates the passage of girls from childhood into adulthood. Girls between the ages of eight and ten, attired in pretty dresses, their hands painted with henna, are initiated into the rituals of fasting. They are presented with a sewing needle dipped in honey and a thimble full of milk, symbolizing their imminent entry into womanhood.

Aïd el Fitr celebrates the end of Ramadan. On that morning, family and friends gather around a table laden with appetizing foods, tea and delicacies. Alms are given to the poor. Cakes prepared in advance are handed around. The festival of the day of Achoura affirms the obligation of all Muslims to pay *zakkat*, alms to the poor. Meals start early in the morning and consist of *bellya* couscous with lamb's tail preserved in salt since Aïd el Kebir, *zemmeta*, an orange-flower water and honey semolina, *krachels*, sweet bread rolls with sesame and dried fruits. Achoura is also a children's festival when they receive small presents consisting of dates, nuts and dried fruits. Mouloud commemorates the birth of the Prophet. An opportunity to feast on hearty breakfasts and dishes of couscous, this is a period for popular Muslim gatherings around the tombs of holy men. Aïd el Kebir (see page 50) provides an ideal opportunity to cook a whole sheep on a spit over a barbecue.

Family celebrations are also religious affairs that mark important stages throughout the cycle of life. The essentials of all rituals remain the same, although variations exist from region to region. On the seventh day after birth, a child is given a forename, while the men of the household slaughter a sacrificial lamb. A large number of guests squeeze together around the table for festive meals. Even the smallest events of childhood are cause for a celebratory meal: the day of weaning, the first tooth, circumcision, are all occasions when the child is king for the day. As for marriage ceremonies and feasting, this involves cooks in a flurry of activity for several days in advance, where great quantities of sugar, flour, jars of oil, pyramids of gazelle's horns, buttered *ghribas*, *feqqas* and *haloua* a mountain of nougat, are central to the festive preparations. Huge and protracted celebrations take place in both families, consecrating the future life of the newly-weds.

Imperial City

مدينة إمبراطورية

فاس

of Fès

The imperial city of Fès has been a cultural melting pot of Arabs, Berbers, Jews and Andalusians for several centuries and to this day the city remains the acme of urban existence. Located amid fertile, agricultural, flat, open country, and at the crossroads of major trading routes, the city has expanded, while attracting numerous migrant populations and traders drawn from all over the

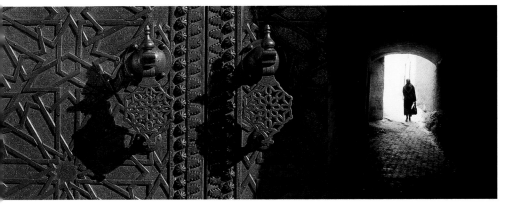

LEFT
Detail of copper engraving, on the doors of the Royal Palace of Fès, featuring huge door-knockers.

RIGHT
The medina is a maze of alleyways exposed to the sky, and covered dead-ends leading to individual houses.

Maghreb. For many years Fès was the link port for caravans crossing the Sahara desert as they travelled through Morocco from Tafilalet to the Mediterranean. Morocco's oldest imperial city was founded in the late eighth century by Idriss I, a native of Baghdad, who was recognized as a religious and political leader by the Berbers of the region. Forced to flee from Andalusia by the Ommeyades at the beginning of the ninth century, several thousand Muslim and Jewish families installed themselves on the right bank of the *oued* or *wadi* (seasonal river) of Fès. Six years later, two thousand Arabs fleeing Kairouan, in Tunisia, also took refuge within the imperial city, occupying its left bank. Descendants of these two great cultural families of the Cordue and Kairouan era, these refugees played a major role in the development of Fès. Invaded time and again by the Berbers, the Fatimids, and

the Ommeyades, the imperial city experienced times of great prosperity, but it also witnessed some darker periods. Over the centuries, Fès remained the staunch religious and cultural capital of the realm and was revered by all the great sultans. During the twelfth century, under the rule of the Almohad Empire, which stretched from Tripoli to the Atlantic Ocean and from southern Spain to the Sudan, some of the greatest scholars and artists of the time flocked to Fès, congregating around the city's Kairouine Mosque. In the fourteenth century, the Merinids elevated art, culture and savoir-faire to new heights. If the chroniclers of the day are to be believed the cuisine of that period offered great diversity, as well as sumptuous visual presentation.

Arabs and Jews fled the *Reconquista* (the Christian re-conquest of Spain) en masse and settled in Fès, Rabat and Tétouan, bringing with them eight centuries of culinary tradition. Fès is the symbol of this secular cultural know-how. Everything there is somehow more refined than elsewhere. The social conventions in Fès are also the most deeply ingrained, for example a strong sense of business acumen and a concern for perfection, all characteristics that, to this day, continue to motivate the Fassi population (inhabitants of Fès). In times when the middle classes had yet to desert the city to profit from the economic and political metropolises of Casablanca and Rabat, families would think nothing of entertaining 30 or 40 people at a time for sumptuous lunches. Exposed to the outside world for so many years, Fès today is closing in upon itself, jealously retaining within its walls part of the culture and history of Morocco. In the medina, behind any one of the facades punctuated by austere studded doors and

RIGHT AND ABOVE
The ancient city of Fès remains the intellectual, religious and artistic capital of Morocco. In the alleyways of the medina, anonymous doors in tall facades hide ancient fondouks *(inns and storehouses), mosques, sumptuous* medersas *(former student hostels associated with the mosques) and superb residences.*

narrow windows, flower-covered patios filled with trees lead to splendid interiors, decorated with *zelliges* (mosaics) and stucco. There, hidden in the secretive environment of its kitchens, culinary traditions endure. Today, throughout the whole of Morocco, Fassi cuisine lays proud claim to its numerous recipes – an artistry that rests upon the painstaking preparation of much sought-after

hearts carefully removed, broad (fava) beans, peas and cardoons. Then there are vegetable tagines and also fruit tagines. Fès has inherited the refinement of Andalusian cuisine. Other marvellous recipes bear testimony to this tradition: sweet-and-sour chicken couscous, accompanied by onions, chickpeas (garbanzos) and honey; stuffed chicken or pigeon couscous, with almonds, currants, onions and honey; red marrow (zucchini) couscous with raisins. In times gone by, *khlii*, a conserve of lamb, beef and camel, was prepared every year in all the great houses of Fès. Served with lentils or courgettes (zucchini), crumbled over eggs or accompanied by a tomato sauce, it makes a suitable replacement for fresh meat in a couscous. Sun dried and carved into strips, the meat is soaked in water overnight. Next day the fat is rubbed with salt and then chopped. The meat is mixed with crushed garlic, coriander and caraway, covered with water and brought to the boil. Four hours of simmering are required for the water to evaporate completely. Olive oil is added at the end of the cooking process. Covered in melted fat, the meat can be stored in preserving jars for up to two years. Fassi cuisine is equally appropriate for a celebration dish, with *mrouzia* served at the time of Aïd el Kebir. Lamb-based, with raisins, honey and almonds, this dish is flavoured with ras-el-hanout, literally 'the top of the shop'. Skilfully prepared, this assortment of the best spices varies according to the region and the grocer's secrets. This particular blend consists of about 27 spices, including cardamom, maniguette, nutmeg, mace, Spanish fly, cayenne pepper, turmeric, ginger, black pepper, white ginger, dried chillies, also cinnamon, cloves, curry, galanga and iris. Today, numerous families have moved

LEFT
The serwal *(wide trousers),* chamir *(vest) and* jellaba *(long tunic) are the traditional clothes of the urban man.*

RIGHT
The red fez, cylindrical with a flat top and a black tassel, is worn daily by many men in Morocco.

flavours; starting with the tagine, a typical dish of Fassi origin that blends spicy aromas with sweetness.

Smothered in a smooth creamy sauce, meat or poultry is covered with vegetables or fruit. Lamb or beef tagines, where the meat has been browned or marinated, offer fabulous diversity, the most famous of which is tagine of lamb with prunes, which was originally a dish cooked for celebrations. Spices and black pepper contrast with the sweet taste of prunes, cinnamon and honey. A dish for special occasions, pigeon pastilla would have been brought to Fès by the Andalusians, just like tagine tfaya, prepared from a lamb, chicken or beef base, flavoured with ginger, saffron, coriander (cilantro), garlic and onion and served with hard-boiled (hard-cooked) eggs and blanched toasted almonds. Fassi tagines follow the seasons. In spring, they are filled with wild artichokes, with the from Fès to the Atlantic. The medina has become popular with the middle classes, as has its cuisine. Traversed by donkeys loaded with merchandise, the best means of transport in the maze of alleyways, the medina is traditionally the centre for crafts – joinery, copperware, leather, weaving, pottery and ceramics. It is also a place where you can always find something to eat.

Eating outside the home is not common practice because there are few restaurants that can compete with home cooking, except for luxury establishments. In their stalls, the budget restaurateurs, who appreciate their customers' high culinary standards, recommend meat of impeccable freshness – despite its 'basic' storage conditions – or the smoothest of creamy tagines. The stalls offer *bessara*, dried

beans cooked with cumin and paprika, green salads topped with huge onion rings, hard-boiled (hard-cooked) eggs with salt and cumin, sheep's heads, calves' feet, the main specialities of street cuisine. On glowing charcoal braziers, skewers of meats coated in cumin are lined up ready to slide into a lump of *kesra* so that none of the spicy taste is lost. Mint flavours merge with the aromas of tagines cooking on *kanouns*. Barrows trundle past, some loaded with fruit, vegetables or nougat, others laden with pots of cooked snails.

At every street corner, women sell *beghrirs*, pancakes, while the smell of sizzling doughnuts tantalizes the nostrils. With dexterity, the doughnut seller forms crown-shaped *sfenjs* from a bowl of white dough, which puffs up when cooked and turns a golden colour. From his basin of hot oil, he fishes out the *sfenjs* with a hook and threads them on a palm frond.

LEFT
The palaces, mosques and medersas of Fès remain immersed in their exceptional Arab-Andalusian artistic heritage. The coloured mosaics, (zelliges) carved stucco, sculpted and painted wood, blend perfectly in all the decorative arts.

ABOVE
The curved dagger, koumiya, *in a silver sheath, is an item of male finery, more a social symbol than a weapon. It is always worn on the left side.*

بيض جيد

Fès el Bali, the old town, contains souks grouped by activities within its walls. Through one of the medina's main commercial arteries, extend the Souk el Attarine featuring the warm colours and spellbinding aromas of spices. On display in bulk, these conical heaps of ground spices and herbs are bought by weight. In addition, henna in leaf and powder form can be found, as well as kohl, (eye-liner for women), and ghassoul, clay used as shampoo.

RIGHT
Cinnamon is sold in the form of small pieces of fragrant bark.

Carrot, orange and cinnamon salad

The huge variety of
fresh fruits and
vegetables, available
all year round from
the markets, is one of
the main attractions
of Moroccan cuisine.

This recipe can be made
using other vegetables,
such as boiled, diced
beetroot (beet), to which
a teaspoon of white
vinegar has been added.
Alternatively, use
peeled, grated cucumbers
with a little added
vinegar and thyme.

SERVES 6
PREPARATION: 30 MINUTES
CHILLING: 2 HOURS

750 G (1½ LB) CARROTS, ABOUT 12
3 LARGE ORANGES
300 G (SCANT 1½ CUPS) CASTER (SUPERFINE) SUGAR
1 TABLESPOON GROUND CINNAMON
1 TEASPOON ORANGE-FLOWER WATER
PINCH OF SALT
TO GARNISH:
MINT LEAVES AND ICING (CONFECTIONERS') SUGAR (OPTIONAL)

Grate the carrots.
Remove the pith and dice the flesh of 2 oranges.
Place the grated carrot, diced orange, sugar, cinnamon, orange-flower water, salt, and the juice only of the third orange, in a salad bowl and toss thoroughly. Chill for at least 2 hours.
Serve garnished with finely chopped mint, and dusted with icing (confectioners') sugar at the last minute, if you like.

Bekkoula (marsh mallow leaves)

Sold by the bunch, marsh mallow is a vegetable that belongs to the spinach family, and is only available in Moroccan markets during the winter months and early springtime.

This recipe can be made using spinach, Chinese cabbage leaves, broccoli, or even green cabbage.

SERVES 6

PREPARATION TIME: 30 MINUTES

COOKING TIME: 40 MINUTES

1 KG (2 LB) MARSH MALLOW LEAVES

3 GARLIC CLOVES, SLICED

3 TABLESPOONS OLIVE OIL

½ BUNCH OF FLAT LEAF PARSLEY, FINELY CHOPPED

½ BUNCH OF CORIANDER (CILANTRO), FINELY CHOPPED

1 TEASPOON GROUND CUMIN

½ TEASPOON MILD GROUND PIMENTO

½ TEASPOON GROUND PEPPER

SALT

2 TABLESPOONS LIME JUICE

TO GARNISH:

½ PRESERVED LEMON (OPTIONAL)

12 GREEN OLIVES (OPTIONAL)

Rinse the marsh mallow leaves and remove the stalks. Using a knife, finely chop the leaves and steam with the sliced garlic for about 20 minutes; drain thoroughly.

Heat the oil in a heavy pan, add the marsh mallow leaves and garlic and reduce over medium heat, stirring constantly, to prevent the mixture from sticking to the pan.

Add the parsley, coriander (cilantro), spices, and salt to taste.

Continue cooking until all the liquid from the marsh mallow has evaporated. Sprinkle with lime juice.

Serve cold, garnished with slices of preserved lemon and whole olives, if you like.

Pastilla (almond and pigeon [squab] pie)

SERVES 8
PREPARATION TIME: 1½ HOURS
COOKING TIME: 1½ HOURS

6–8 PIGEONS (SQUAB), BREAST MEAT ONLY

100 G (SCANT ½ CUP) BUTTER

OLIVE OIL

500 G (1 LB) ONIONS, FINELY CHOPPED
(ABOUT 2 CUPS)

½ TEASPOON GROUND GINGER

½ TEASPOON GROUND PEPPER

750 ML (3 CUPS) WATER

GROUND CORIANDER (TO TASTE)

½ PACKET SAFFRON, OR PINCH OF THREADS

1 TABLESPOON GROUND CINNAMON

200 G (1 CUP) CASTER (SUPERFINE) SUGAR

12 EGGS

LARGE BUNCH OF FLAT LEAF PARSLEY, CHOPPED

250 G (2 CUPS) BLANCHED ALMONDS

5 FILO PASTRY SHEETS (OR 12 SHEETS BRIK)

MELTED BUTTER FOR SEALING AND GLAZING

TO GARNISH:

ICING (CONFECTIONERS') SUGAR AND
GROUND CINNAMON

BELOW

Throughout the ages, Moroccan cuisine has been the preserve of women, where knowledge is handed down by word of mouth from mother to daughter. Regional and family traditions persist as closely guarded culinary secrets.

FACING PAGE

A beautifully decorated pastilla.

Slice the pigeon meat into bite-size pieces. Heat the butter and oil in a large pan, add the onions and cook until they soften. Stir in the ginger, pepper and pour in the water. Add the pigeon (squab) meat and mix well. Partially cover the pan and simmer over medium heat for 30 minutes.

Remove from the heat, take out the pieces of pigeon (squab) and set aside. Add the coriander, saffron, cinnamon and sugar to the pan. Reduce the sauce and break the eggs into it, one at a time. Continue cooking, for 5 minutes, stirring constantly with a wooden spoon, making sure that the mixture does not stick to the base of the pan. Remove from the heat, stir in the parsley, and set aside to cool.

Preheat the oven to 180°C (350°F), Gas Mark 4.

Heat a little oil in a pan, add the almonds and cook until light brown. Drain on kitchen paper (paper towels) and chop.

Cover the base of a greased 23-cm (9-inch) pie tin (pan) with 6 half-sheets of filo overlapping the edges generously. Place a folded sheet in the middle, for extra strength. Arrange half the almonds on the pastry case (pie shell), pour in the onion and egg mixture, add the meat and top with a layer of the remaining almonds. Draw together and seal the pastry edges, cover with 2 half-sheets and tuck in under the rim. Seal and glaze the pie with melted butter. Bake for 45–60 minutes.

Transfer the pie to a serving dish and garnish with alternating lines of sugar and cinnamon, radiating from the centre.

Aubergine (eggplant) zaalouk

Serves 4

Preparation time: 15 minutes

Overall cooking time: 40 minutes

4 large aubergines (eggplant)

½ lemon

2 garlic cloves, crushed

salt

3 tablespoons oil

1 tablespoon tomato purée (paste)

½ teaspoon ground mild pimento

ground cumin (to taste)

½ teaspoon ground pepper

½ bunch of flat leaf parsley, finely chopped

½ bunch of coriander (cilantro), finely chopped

lemon juice, to taste

Rinse the aubergines (eggplant) and remove the skin from two of them. Dice the flesh of all 4 and place in a steamer with the ½ lemon for its flavour (do not squeeze), the garlic and a little salt. Cook for 25 minutes. Remove from the heat and take out the ½ lemon. Drain the aubergines (eggplant) in a colander, pressing down hard to remove the liquid.

Heat the oil in a pan and stir in the tomato purée (paste). Add the aubergine (eggplant) and garlic mixture to the pan. Cook to reduce, stirring constantly.

When all the liquid has evaporated, add the spices, parsley and coriander (cilantro). Mix well and sprinkle with a dash of lemon juice, to taste.

This dish is eaten cold. It can be stored in the refrigerator.

Note:

Cooking the aubergines (eggplant) with lemon juice is not recommended as it prevents them from browning. In addition, cooking in a steamer avoids the charred aftertaste, commonly associated with baking aubergines (eggplant) in the oven.

Lentil zaalouk

Serves 6
Preparation time: 10 minutes
Cooking time: 25 minutes

500 g (2 cups) lentils
Olive oil
4 garlic cloves, crushed
1 small bunch of flat leaf parsley,
finely chopped
1 bunch of coriander (cilantro),
finely chopped
1 teaspoon mild ground pimento
Pinch of ground cumin
White wine vinegar
Salt
Pepper

Simmer the lentils in a pan in about 1 litre (4 cups) water, salt and pepper, over medium heat for about 15 minutes or until the lentils are cooked through but still hold their shape. Drain and rinse the lentils under cold water.

Heat the olive oil in a pan, add the lentils, garlic, parsley, coriander (cilantro) and pimento.

Cook until the lentils are reduced to a pulp, add the cumin and a dash of white wine vinegar and check the seasoning.

Cauliflower zaalouk

Serves 6
Preparation time: 10 minutes
Cooking time: 30 minutes

500 g (1 lb) cauliflower
4 garlic cloves, crushed
Olive oil
1 teaspoon mild ground pimento
1 small bunch of flat leaf parsley,
finely chopped
1 bunch of coriander (cilantro),
finely chopped
White wine vinegar
Pinch of ground cumin
Salt

Carrot zaalouk

Serves 6
Preparation time: 15 minutes
Cooking time: 30 minutes

500 g (1 lb) carrots, about 8
4 garlic cloves
1 small bunch of flat leaf parsley,
finely chopped
1 bunch of coriander (cilantro),
finely chopped
1 teaspoon mild ground pimento
1 tablespoon olive oil
Pinch of ground cumin
White wine vinegar
Salt

Chop the carrots and cook in a pan of salted water, with the garlic cloves, over medium heat for 10 minutes.

Drain the carrots, pick out the garlic and set aside. Put the carrots in a bowl and mash with a fork. Reduce the garlic to a purée, then fold into the carrots, add the parsley, coriander (cilantro) and pimento and mix well.

Heat the olive oil in clean pan, add the carrot mixture and quickly cook, stirring, into a purée. Finally, stir in the cumin and a dash of white wine vinegar and adjust the seasoning to taste.

Divide the cauliflower into small florets, place in a steamer and cook until tender. Mash with a fork.

Mix the garlic with the oil and add the cauliflower, pimento, parsley and coriander (cilantro). Mix well together.

Serve, warm or chilled, sprinkled with a dash of white wine vinegar and a pinch of cumin. Adjust seasoning to taste.

FACING PAGE
Cauliflower purée
The term 'zaalouk', in Moroccan cuisine, is not limited to aubergine purée, but can be used loosely, and with a little imagination, to describe all other types of purées.

الزيتون OLIVES

Olive trees with their silver foliage grow in tightly packed rows, throughout the Marrakech, Beni Mellal and Agadir regions, and are particularly abundant in Rif, in the north of the country. They require minimal cultivation, with roots extending from their gnarled trunks, firmly embedded in the stony terrain. Fruit of the land, green, purple and black olives are harvested from November through to December. The bulk of the crop is destined for the production of oil at the hundreds of *maasras*, oil-mills, dotted around the country (see description, page 141). Any surplus is sold in the souks, where olives are displayed in 'pyramids', according to their method of preparation and their usage in regional cooking: olives for tagines, piquant olives, with red pimento, purple olives, with a pungent flavour... To produce olives preserved in bitter orange, purple olives are pitted and blended with the flesh of crushed salted oranges and left to steep in water for at least three weeks. Green or purple olives are suitable for making into a 'pulp'. The crushed olives are left to steep for eight days in water, which is renewed daily, to remove their bitter taste. They are then consumed on their own or in a tagine. Black olives that have been covered in salt and blanched release a blackish juice over the course of several weeks. Rinsed in water, sun-dried, then immersed in oil, they can be stored for a long time in preserving jars.

Black, green or deep purple, steeped in herbs, seasoned with chilli, or preserved in bitter orange, the range of olives sold at market varies according to their specialities.

Chekchouka

Serves 4
Preparation time: 30 minutes
Cooking time: 30 minutes

4 green (bell) peppers
4 tomatoes
1 tablespoon groundnut (peanut) oil
1 garlic clove, crushed
salt
½ bunch of coriander (cilantro),
finely chopped
½ bunch of flat leaf parsley,
finely chopped
1 teaspoon ground cumin
½ teaspoon mild ground pimento
1 tablespoon olive oil

Rinse the (bell) peppers, dry carefully and place them under the grill (broiler), turning them to make sure that they are grilled (broiled) on all sides. When the skins are evenly browned, remove from the grill (broiler) and when cool enough to handle, cut open, deseed and dice the flesh.

Place the tomatoes in a bowl and pour over boiling water to cover. Leave for 1–2 minutes, drain, pierce with a sharp knife, peel off the skins and dice the flesh. Heat the groundnut (peanut) oil in a heavy pan; add the garlic, tomatoes and salt. Simmer over medium heat until all the liquid has evaporated. Stir in the (bell) peppers and simmer for a little longer.

When is well blended, add the coriander (cilantro), parsley, cumin, pimento and olive oil. Cook for 5 minutes over low heat and adjust the seasoning to taste. Serve cold.

Green (bell) pepper and tomato salad

Serves 6
Preparation time: 30 minutes

2 green (bell) peppers
4 large tomatoes
½ preserved lemon, for garnish
1 teaspoon chopped parsley
2 tablespoons olive oil
1 tablespoon lemon juice
½ teaspoon ground cumin
1 garlic clove, crushed
salt

Grill (broil) the (bell) peppers, rinse in cold water, deseed and dice. Skin the tomatoes as described on page 34, deseed and dice. Remove the pulp from the preserved lemon and discard. Cut the rind into thin strips. Combine the (bell) peppers, tomatoes, parsley, oil, lemon juice, cumin, garlic and salt to taste in a salad bowl and toss thoroughly.
Serve, garnished with the strips of preserved lemon.

Lettuce and orange salad

Serves 4
Preparation time: 20 minutes

1 whole lettuce or 2 lettuce hearts
3 oranges
2 tablespoons lemon juice
pinch of salt
2 tablespoons sugar
1 teaspoon orange-flower water
1 teaspoon groundnut (peanut) oil

Rinse the lettuce, drain and cut across the leaves into strips. Cut the skin and pith from 2 oranges and slice into rounds. Place the lettuce and orange in a salad bowl, sprinkle with the lemon juice and the juice from the remaining orange. Add the salt, sugar, orange-flower water and oil. Toss gently to mix the flavours and serve immediately.

Lettuce and orange salad can also be made using young, fresh horseradish leaves cut into thin strips, or watercress and rocket (arugula), instead of lettuce.

Kefta (minced [ground] meat) briouats

SERVES 6
PREPARATION TIME: 1 HOUR
COOKING TIME: 30 MINUTES

500 G (4 CUPS) MINCED (GROUND) MEAT OF CHOICE
3 ONIONS, FINELY CHOPPED
1 SPRIG OF CORIANDER (CILANTRO), FINELY CHOPPED
1 BUNCH OF PARSLEY, FINELY CHOPPED
100 ML (SCANT ½ CUP) OIL
6 EGGS
1 TEASPOON GROUND CINNAMON
1 TEASPOON PEPPER
PINCH OF SAFFRON
1 TEASPOON SALT
6 SHEETS FILO PASTRY (12 SHEETS BRIK)
OIL FOR DEEP-FRYING

In a bowl, thoroughly mix together the meat, one-third of the onions, the coriander (cilantro) and half the parsley.

Heat the oil in a large pan, add the remainder of the onions and cook over low heat to soften. Add the rest of the parsley. Reduce the heat and break the eggs into the onions, one at a time.

Cook for 20 seconds, stirring constantly with a wooden spoon. Add the meat stuffing, cinnamon, pepper, saffron, and salt. Mix well.

Cook, stirring constantly, for 8–10 minutes or until the mixture is cooked through, but not over-cooked.

Cut each filo pastry sheet into 4 rectangles (25 x 11.5 cm/ 10 x 4½ inches). Fill and fold the briouats as described on page 37.

Deep-fry the briouats as described in the recipe for Cheese and pistachio briouats on this page.

Cheese and pistachio briouats

MAKES 12
PREPARATION TIME: 45 MINUTES
COOKING TIME: 5 MINUTES EACH SIDE

150 G (5 OZ) SOFT SHEEP'S MILK CHEESE
2 TEASPOONS OLIVE OIL
PINCH OF CASTER (SUPERFINE) SUGAR
3 PINCHES OF GROUND PEPPER
3 SHEETS FILO PASTRY (4 SHEETS BRIK)
OIL FOR DEEP-FRYING
50 G (½ CUP) SHELLED PISTACHIOS, CHOPPED

Crumble the cheese into a salad bowl. Add the oil, sugar and pepper and mix lightly to avoid forming a paste.

Cut each filo pastry sheet into 4 rectangles (25 x 11.5 cm/ 10 x 4½ inches). Fill and fold the briouats as described on page 37.

Heat 5 cm (2 inches) of oil in a deep pan and deep-fry the briouats until they are golden brown all over (about 5 minutes on each side).

Serve warm. Sprinkle with the pistachios, just before serving.

Despite the advent of modern cooking techniques, Moroccan women remain faithful to traditional methods, kneading bread every morning and preparing innumerable sweet delicacies with great skill.

How to fold briouats

If using filo pastry, cut the sheets to the size indicated in the recipe, following the manufacturer's instructions for handling the pastry to prevent it from drying out.

Place a small portion of the filling on one corner of the base of the rectangle, 2.5 cm (I inch) above the edge. Fold the other corner over the filling to make a triangle. Continue to fold from left to right, with as light a touch as possible, until the pastry strip is used up, tucking in the left-over flap at the end to prevent the briouat from coming apart during cooking.

If using brik, spread a round sheet of brik pastry on a flat work surface (counter), cut in half to form a semicircle, and then in half again lengthways, to form a strip. Fill and fold as described above.

The process of folding briouats requires considerable patience. Typically triangle-shaped, they can also be formed into rectangles and sealed at both ends, or even formed into little cylinders.

Semolina soup with aniseed

FACING PAGE

Caraway (Carum carvi), *a plant of Asian origins, is often confused with cumin* (Cuminum cyminum). *Its bitter-sweet flavour more closely resembles that of aniseed and it is used to add aroma to soups and bread.*

SERVES 8

PREPARATION TIME: 10 MINUTES

COOKING TIME: 30 MINUTES

1 LITRE (4 CUPS) WATER

250 G (1⅔ CUPS) SEMOLINA

1 LITRE (4 CUPS) BOILING MILK

1 TEASPOON GROUND ANISEED

1 TABLESPOON ORANGE-FLOWER WATER (OPTIONAL)

1 TABLESPOON CASTER (SUPERFINE) SUGAR (OPTIONAL)

SALT (OPTIONAL)

Bring the water to the boil in a pan. Pour in the semolina in a steady stream, stirring constantly to prevent lumps from forming. Return to the boil, reduce the heat and cook, stirring constantly, for 15 minutes.

Add the boiling milk and ground aniseed and continue cooking for a further 5 minutes. Depending on preferences, you can add the orange-flower water, caster (superfine) sugar and salt to taste.

Mint and caraway soup

SERVES 8

PREPARATION TIME: 30 MINUTES

COOKING TIME: 15 MINUTES

ABOVE

Known in Morocco, as beç beç aniseed is renowned for its medicinal properties. Ground to heighten their flavour, aniseed grains aid digestion.

The method used to prepare this soup is the same as for harira soup (see recipe page 40). The ingredients are the same apart from substituting a bunch of mint for the coriander (cilantro) and adding a pinch of gum arabic (also known as gum acacia) and a teaspoon of caraway seeds.

This soup is enjoyed, in summer, on the morning of Aïd el Kebir (the festival when sheep are sacrificed, see page 50), as an accompaniment for steamed lamb's head. This refreshing soup is good for the digestion.

Harira

This thick soup signals the end of the fast of Ramadan. Harira soups are rich and nourishing and made from a variety of dried and fresh vegetables, beef, chicken wings, calves or chicken liver, poultry gizzards and thickened with *taddouira*. On certain occasions, harira is consumed for breakfast, particularly on days following holidays.

SERVES 8
PREPARATION TIME: 30 MINUTES
COOKING TIME: 1½ HOURS

100 G (SCANT ½ CUP) CHICKPEAS (GARBANZO BEANS), SOAKED OVERNIGHT
OIL
1 LARGE ONION, THINLY SLICED
CHICKEN GIBLETS OR MEAT, DICED
½ BUNCH OF PARSLEY, CHOPPED
1½ BUNCHES OF CORIANDER (CILANTRO), CHOPPED
½ TEASPOON GROUND GINGER
2 CINNAMON STICKS
1 PINCH OF GROUND SAFFRON
1 TABLESPOON SALT
1 TEASPOON GROUND PEPPER
100 G (SCANT ½ CUP) BROWN LENTILS, RINSED
4 TABLESPOONS FLOUR
1 TABLESPOON TOMATO PURÉE (PASTE)
1 LITRE (4 CUPS) COLD WATER
100 G (⅔ CUP) BOILED RICE
DATES
LEMON JUICE

Drain the chickpeas (garbanzos). Heat a little oil in a large pan and soften the onion. Add the meat, parsley, I bunch of coriander (cilantro), the spices, chickpeas (garbanzos), salt and pepper and simmer for 30 minutes. Stir in the lentils and simmer for 30 minutes more or until both the chickpeas (garbanzos) and lentils are tender.

To prepare the *taddouira* stock: Blend the flour and tomato purée (paste) in the measured water, add the remaining chopped coriander (cilantro).

Stir the rice into the soup and gradually pour in the *taddouira* stock, stirring constantly until all the surface froth has disappeared. Simmer to thicken.

Serve accompanied by dates and lemon juice in separate bowls.

To the sound of the first sirens that herald the end of the month fast of Ramadan, steaming harira graces tables throughout the kingdom. In this nourishing soup, made from a variety of ingredients, dried vegetables dominate.

Harira ouazzania

The city of Ouezzane (also known as Wazzan), in northeast Morocco, is situated in the foothills of the Rif mountain range, where vines, olive trees and fig trees are cultivated. This town boasts a rich cultural heritage, steeped in tradition. The *Chorfas* of Ouezzane are one of the oldest families in Morocco.
Ouezzane is also a place of Jewish pilgrimage, made famous, worldwide, by Rabbi Amran of Ouezzane.

SERVES 6
PREPARATION TIME: 30 MINUTES
COOKING TIME: 1½ HOURS

1 TABLESPOON OIL

2 LARGE ONIONS, CHOPPED

250 G (8 OZ) BEEF, DICED

1 TABLESPOON SALT

100 G (SCANT ½ CUP) BROWN LENTILS, RINSED

¼ GREEN CABBAGE

1 TEASPOON GROUND SAFFRON

½ TEASPOON GROUND PEPPER

100 G (¾ CUP) FRESH BROAD (FAVA) BEANS

1 BUNCH OF CORIANDER (CILANTRO), CHOPPED

½ BUNCH OF PARSLEY, CHOPPED

4 TURNIPS, DICED

4 TABLESPOONS FLOUR

1 TABLESPOON TOMATO PURÉE (PASTE)

LEMON JUICE

FIGS

Heat the oil in a large pan and soften the onions. Add the meat, salt and 1 litre (4 cups) of cold water. Bring to the boil and boil gently for 20 minutes.

Steep the lentils in boiling water for 5 minutes to release their brown colour, and drain. Blanch the cabbage for 5 minutes and cut into thin strips.

Add the saffron, pepper, broad (fava) beans, coriander (cilantro), parsley, lentils and 500 ml (generous 2 cups) of boiling water to the onions and meat. Stir well and cook for 15 minutes. Add the shredded cabbage and turnips and cook until tender.

While the soup is in its final stages of cooking, prepare the *taddouira* to thicken the soup.

Using a whisk, blend the flour and tomato purée (paste) in 1 litre (4 cups) of cold water.

Gradually pour the stock into the soup, stirring gently all the time; continue cooking until the white froth on the surface has completely disappeared and the soup thickens.

Adjust seasoning to taste and serve accompanied by lemon juice and figs in separate bowls.

LEFT
A round, home-made loaf of bread, cut into triangular pieces, is always placed on the dining table as a symbol of sharing and friendship.

COPPERWARE لوازم الطبخ نحاسية صفراء

In the vast souks of Fès or Marrakech, the sound of copper being hammered out reveals the intensely physical nature of the work involved; it also indicates the whereabouts of the metalworkers' quarter.

Constantly labouring in high temperatures, craftsmen work the reddish-brown coloured copper, the gleaming yellow brass – from copper and zinc ore – and nickel silver, an alloy of copper, zinc and nickel.

Vast cauldrons take shape under the pounding of hammers that flatten and mould the copper. These heavy metal cooking pots serve, among other uses, as vessels for cooking lamb and mutton on festive occasions.

The hands of these craftsmen create glistening plates of engraved brass, decorated in geometric or floral patterns; bulbous teapots with pointed lids; braziers with decorative scalloped sides in ornamental openwork; perfume burners, engraved with Islamic motifs; wash-stands with false bottoms, made of brass; elegant ewers with long tapering spouts; boxes for storing sugar…

Hand-decorated using a *burin* (engraving tool), before pressing, the most exquisite pieces are engraved with the aid of styli, guided by the skilled hands of true craftsmen.

Plain, stamped, or engraved with motifs inspired by Islam, round copper and brass plates are plentiful in all Moroccan homes.

Wash-stands, tass (basins), and elegant ewers made from copper or silver plate are still offered to diners to wash their hands before and after important traditional meals.

Samovar, ewer, plate, candlestick…nickel silver takes pride of place among Moroccan furnishings, but is less evident in the country's architectural decoration.

After gold and silver, copper is considered to be the finest metal and is used for the pointed lids that keep tagines warm on festive occasions or for protecting the traditional round loaves from dust and flies.

White turnip and lentil tagine

Fresh and sun-drenched, Moroccan vegetables are so flavoursome that they are often eaten as a meal in themselves, in the form of many different types of tagines.

SERVES 6
PREPARATION TIME: 15 MINUTES
COOKING TIME: 1½ HOURS

2 TABLESPOONS OIL
1 ONION, CHOPPED
2 GARLIC CLOVES, CRUSHED
250 (8 OZ) BEEF, DICED
500 ML (GENEROUS 2 CUPS) BOILING WATER
1 TEASPOON GROUND CUMIN
½ TEASPOON GROUND MILD CHILLI POWDER
PINCH OF SAFFRON
½ BUNCH OF PARSLEY, FINELY CHOPPED
½ BUNCH OF CORIANDER (CILANTRO),
FINELY CHOPPED
500 G (2 CUPS) GREEN LENTILS
1 KG (2 LB) TURNIPS
SALT

Heat the oil in a large pan or flameproof casserole and soften the onion with the garlic. Add the meat and cook, stirring and turning, until brown. Cover with the boiling water; add the spices and herbs and return to the boil. Simmer over medium heat for about 1 hour.

Meanwhile, steep the lentils in boiling water; drain and rinse thoroughly several times to remove any brown colour. Peel and dice the turnips.

When the meat is nearly cooked, add the lentils and turnips and simmer for 15 minutes. The turnips will produce some liquid but add more boiling water if the tagine appears to be dry.

This recipe can be made with or without meat, or with confit of duck.

Vegetable tagine

SERVES 4
PREPARATION TIME: 30 MINUTES
COOKING TIME: 30 MINUTES

2 TABLESPOONS OLIVE OIL

1 LARGE ONION, SLICED INTO ROUNDS

3 POTATOES, PEELED AND QUARTERED

2 COURGETTES (ZUCCHINI), CUT LENGTHWAYS

2 TOMATOES, SLICED INTO FAIRLY THICK ROUNDS

2 CARROTS, CUT LENGTHWAYS AND BLANCHED

1 BUNCH OF PARSLEY, CHOPPED

1 BUNCH OF CORIANDER (CILANTRO), CHOPPED

PINCH OF THYME

1 TEASPOON SALT

1 TEASPOON GROUND PEPPER

1 TEASPOON GROUND CUMIN

Heat the oil in a tagine or flameproof casserole and soften the onion. Add a layer of potatoes on top, then the courgettes (zucchini), tomatoes and finally the carrots.

Sprinkle with parsley, coriander (cilantro) and thyme, then the salt, pepper and cumin.

Cover and cook over medium heat. Generally, no additional water is required as there is sufficient liquid from the onions and tomatoes, but keep a check and add a little water if needed.

If you like, a few blanched cauliflower florets may be added (as illustrated in the photograph).

Tfaya couscous with raisins and honey

SERVES 8
PREPARATION TIME: 30 MINUTES
COOKING TIME: 1½ HOURS

5 TABLESPOONS GROUNDNUT (PEANUT) OIL
700 G (1½ LB) BONED LAMB, CUT INTO PIECES
100 G (3½ OZ) ONIONS, CHOPPED, ABOUT 1 CUP
SALT, PEPPER
500 ML (GENEROUS 2 CUPS) WATER
PINCH OF SAFFRON
1 TEASPOON GROUND GINGER
500 G (2⅔ CUPS) FINE GRAIN COUSCOUS
TO GARNISH:
300 G (3½ OZ) ONIONS, THINLY SLICED
4 TABLESPOONS OIL
GROUND CINNAMON
5 TABLESPOONS CLEAR HONEY
250 G (1⅔ CUPS) RAISINS
CASTER (SUPERFINE) SUGAR AND FRESH MILK

NOTE:
A PAN WITH A TIGHTLY FITTING COLANDER, OR A
STEAMER CAN BE USED INSTEAD OF A COUSCOUSIER

Place the oil, meat, onions, salt and pepper in the lower section of a couscousier (see note above), pour in the water and mix well. Bring to the boil, add the saffron and ginger. Adjust the seasoning and add boiling water, as required, during cooking.

Cook the couscous as described on page 150. In a separate pan, prepare the garnish by lightly cooking the onions in the oil. Season with salt and add a good pinch of cinnamon and the honey. Simmer for 30 minutes, stirring gently occasionally, to prevent the onions from forming a purée. Add the raisins 5 minutes before the mixture has finished cooking.

Arrange the couscous in a ring, around the edge of the serving dish, place the meat in the middle and cover with the onion and raisin sauce. Garnish with a dusting of ground cinnamon.

Serve with caster (superfine) sugar and fresh milk in separate bowls.

Milk, turnip and honey couscous

SERVES 8
PREPARATION TIME: 30 MINUTES
COOKING TIME: 1 HOUR

1 KG (5⅓ CUPS) MEDIUM GRAIN COUSCOUS
100 G (SCANT ½ CUP) BUTTER
500 G (1 LB) TURNIPS
500G (1 LB) GREEN BEANS
1 BUNCH OF CORIANDER (CILANTRO), CHOPPED
PEPPER, SALT
PINCH OF SAFFRON
1 LITRE (4 CUPS) MILK

Prepare the couscous (see page 150).
Peel the turnips and cut into cubes.
Trim the beans if stringy and cut into several pieces.
Cook the turnips, beans, coriander (cilantro), pepper, salt and saffron in the water, for 3 minutes.
Boil the milk and blend with the mixture, when cooked.
Serve with the vegetables in the middle of the plate and the couscous in a ring around the edge.

LEFT

In all couscous dishes, the meat and sauce are always arranged in the middle of the dish, while the couscous is placed in a ring around the edge.

Celebratory dishes combine both meat and fruits, with honey as the prime ingredient invariably associated with such sweet-and-sour recipes.

AÏD EL KEBIR

In town and country, the annual celebration, the festival of the sacrificial sheep marks the end of the ritual associated with the pilgrimage to Mecca. This Muslim festival commemorates the sacrifice of Abraham, when his son Ismail was rescued from sacrifice by a ram sent by Allah. Several days beforehand, every home in the land is intent upon acquiring a sheep, the houses are cleansed with water from the fountains, and for the festival, the women adorn themselves with henna. On the morning of the great day, the sheep's throat is slit in the presence of the family. Greatly appreciated, the offal is cooked immediately. The women prepare liver kebabs and the famous *boulfaf*, coated and roasted liver, eaten with salads and washed down with a glass of mint tea. The sheep's meat is not prepared or eaten until the following day, in a tagine, as kebabs, or cooked whole over a barbecue. The typical dish to celebrate Aïd el Kebir is the lamb-based recipe *mrouzia* (honeyed lamb), cooked with raisins, almonds and ras-el-hanout (a classic, rich, spicy recipe that translates literally as the 'top of the shop' or 'storekeeper's choice'. Various methods are used to preserve the meat. Certain cuts are filleted, seasoned and dried, to be used at a later date in the preparation of couscous-based dishes and tagines.

ABOVE
Snow-clad Atlas mountain landscape, where during the harvest months, the mountain dwellers live an almost self-sufficient existence.

RIGHT
This Aïd el Kebir dish resembles a meat conserve which, in the past, could be preserved for several months in an earthenware jar, glazed inside and sealed with oiled paper.

Mrouzia
(a dish prepared on the day after Aïd el Kebir)

SERVES 6
PREPARATION TIME: 30 MINUTES
COOKING TIME: 50 MINUTES

2 GARLIC CLOVES
1 TEASPOON GROUND GINGER
2 TEASPOONS RAS-EL-HANOUT
1 TEASPOON GROUND PEPPER
1 SHOULDER OF LAMB, CUT INTO PIECES ON THE BONE
300 G (10 OZ) ONIONS, CHOPPED, ABOUT 1¼ CUPS
½ TEASPOON GROUND SAFFRON
200 ML (SCANT 1 CUP) OLIVE OIL
200 G (SCANT 1½ CUPS) LARGE JUICY RAISINS
3 TABLESPOONS CLEAR HONEY
150 G (1¼ CUPS) TOASTED ALMONDS, TO GARNISH

Preheat the oven to 180°C (350°F), Gas Mark 4.
Crush the garlic and place in a bowl with the ginger, ras-el-hanout and pepper. Mix in sufficient water to form a paste of a consistency that will coat the meat.
Place the meat in an earthenware casserole or ovenproof glass dish and mix in the onions, saffron and olive oil. Pour in sufficient water to cover.
Cook for 35–40 minutes in the oven, checking the meat from time to time.
As soon as the meat is tender, remove it from the casserole to another pan and add the honey and raisins to the casserole. Allow to caramelize; then return the meat to the sauce. Serve hot, on a dish garnished with toasted almonds.

Sheep shearing only takes place in springtime when the fleeces are lightweight. Washed, graded and carded using basic equipment, then spun, the wool is woven on looms by the Berber womenfolk, according to age-old techniques, shuttling back and forth, row after row, using a hand-held comb-like iron tool to press each layer into place. The wool is then used to make warm blankets, soft rugs, jellabas (traditional hooded tunics) and winter cloaks.

M'hamer shoulder of lamb

SERVES 6

PREPARATION TIME: 30 MINUTES

COOKING TIME: 2 HOURS

1 SHOULDER LAMB

5 TABLESPOONS OLIVE OIL

½ TABLESPOON TOMATO PURÉE (PASTE)

2 LARGE ONIONS, CHOPPED

2 GARLIC CLOVES, SLICED

1 BUNCH OF PARSLEY, CHOPPED

½ BUNCH CORIANDER (CILANTRO), CHOPPED

2 TEASPOONS MILD CHILLI POWDER

1 TEASPOON GROUND CUMIN

RED FOOD COLOURING (OPTIONAL)

1 TABLESPOON SALT

Ask your butcher to cut up the shoulder by severing the bone in six pieces but keeping the meat in one piece. Coat the meat with a paste made from the oil and tomato purée (paste).

Mix the onions, garlic, parsley, coriander (cilantro), chilli powder, cumin, red food colouring (if using) and salt in a large bowl. Add about 400 ml (scant 2 cups) of cold water and mix well. Place the meat in a large pan, pour the sauce over it and bring to the boil over medium heat.

Preheat the oven to 180°C (350°F), Gas Mark 4. Transfer the contents of the pan to a casserole. Turn the shoulder in the sauce to make sure it is thoroughly coated. Cover, and continue cooking, in the oven, for about 1½ hours but keep checking. Remove the lid for the last 10–15 minutes of the cooking time in order to brown the meat. When the meat starts to fall off the bone, remove it from the sauce and reduce the sauce.

If you like, you could serve the whole shoulder as a single piece, on a *taous* plate – large earthenware serving plate – topped with the thick, red sauce. *M'hamer* shoulder may also be served with soufflé potatoes.

Note: To make soufflé potatoes, peel and slice waxy potatoes, wash and pat dry. Deep-fry in oil at 150°C (300°F) for about 5 minutes, drain on kitchen paper (paper towels) and let cool. Deep-fry again at 180°C (350°F) until puffed up and light brown. Drain and serve hot.

ABOVE

Cut into pieces, braised and cooked in a tagine, or roasted whole on a spit over a barbecue, lamb is by far the most popular meat in the Maghreb region. If it is well cooked, lamb can easily be picked off the bone, using one's fingers.

M'hamer chicken tagine

The finished dish could be garnished with halved, hard-boiled (hard-cooked) eggs, sliced fried potatoes or even blanched and toasted almonds.

SERVES 4
PREPARATION TIME: 30 MINUTES
COOKING TIME: 1 HOUR

125 G (½ CUP) BUTTER
125 ML (½ CUP) GROUNDNUT (PEANUT) OIL
1 TEASPOON GROUND GINGER
1 TEASPOON GROUND MILD PIMENTO
2 PINCHES OF SAFFRON
1 TEASPOON GROUND CUMIN
2 LARGE ONIONS, HALVED AND THINLY SLICED
3 GARLIC CLOVES, SLICED
1 BUNCH OF CORIANDER (CILANTRO), CHOPPED
1 FREE-RANGE CHICKEN, CUT INTO 4

Melt half the butter and half the oil in a large pan or flameproof casserole. Add the spices, onions, garlic and coriander (cilantro), stir well and add the chicken pieces. Cover with cold water and bring to the boil over high heat. Continue to boil for a few minutes, then reduce the heat and simmer, checking periodically. When the chicken is cooked through, remove it from the pan and reduce the sauce.

Heat the remainder of the butter and oil in a separate pan and brown the chicken. Serve in a tagine or on a serving dish, topped with the smooth sauce.

Steamed stuffed spring chickens

SERVES 4

PREPARATION TIME: 30 MINUTES

COOKING TIME: 30 MINUTES

2 SPRING CHICKENS OR 1 CHICKEN

2 CHICKEN LIVERS

1 TABLESPOON RICE

1 BUNCH OF MINT

1 BUNCH OF PARSLEY, CHOPPED

3 GARLIC CLOVES, SLICED

2 TABLESPOONS OLIVE OIL

½ TEASPOON GROUND CUMIN

¼ TEASPOON HOT CHILLI POWDER

2 LITRES (4 CUPS) SALTED WATER

2 TABLESPOONS CHOPPED THYME

½ TEASPOON GROUND PEPPER

SALT

Rinse the cavities of the birds and dry with kitchen paper (paper towels). Chop the livers. Boil and drain the rice. Chop 4 sprigs of the mint for the stuffing.

To prepare the stuffing: Put the rice, parsley, mint, garlic, livers, olive oil, cumin and the chilli powder in a bowl, season with salt and mix thoroughly. Stuff the mixture into the cavities.

Place the salted water, thyme and pepper in the base of a couscousier or steamer. Place the poultry in the top section, cover, and steam for about 30 minutes or until the juices run clear when the plumpest part of the meat is pierced with a sharp skewer or the point of a knife. Serve the chickens on a bed of mint, with the stuffing exposed.

The spring chickens should never be cut into pieces but split lengthways just sufficiently to make room for the stuffing. Be careful to make sure that the cumin does not overwhelm the other flavours.

Caramelized onion tagine

SERVES 8

PREPARATION TIME: 30 MINUTES

COOKING TIME: 45 MINUTES

1 KG (2 LB) LAMB SHOULDER MEAT, CUT
INTO CUBES

1 LITRE (4 CUPS) WATER

125 ML (½ CUP) OIL

1 TEASPOON GROUND GINGER

1 SACHET (ENVELOPE) GROUND SAFFRON

½ TEASPOON SALT

½ TEASPOON GROUND PEPPER, TO TASTE

1½ KG (3 LB) ONIONS, CHOPPED, ABOUT
6 CUPS

2 TABLESPOONS CLEAR HONEY

1 TABLESPOON GROUND CINNAMON

2 TABLESPOONS CASTER (SUPERFINE) SUGAR

Place the meat in a large pan with the water, oil, ginger, saffron, salt and pepper and cook over high heat for about 15 minutes.

Add the onions and honey, sprinkle with the cinnamon and sugar, and continue to cook for about another 15 minutes.

Preheat the oven to 200°C (400°F), Gas Mark 6.

As soon as the meat is cooked through, remove from the pan and keep warm.

Reduce the sauce over medium heat until it has thickened. The onions should be golden brown.

Put the meat and the sauce in an ovenproof dish and bake in the oven for about 10–15 minutes to caramelize the onions.

Serve hot.

This recipe can be made using guinea fowl or rabbit instead of lamb.

Quince tagine

SERVES 8

PREPARATION TIME: 30 MINUTES

COOKING TIME: 1¼ HOURS

1 KG (2 LB) MEAT ON THE BONE, SUCH
AS SHOULDER OR LOIN OF LAMB OR VEAL
SHIN (SHANK)

4 TABLESPOONS OLIVE OIL

3 PINCHES OF SAFFRON

3 ONIONS, THINLY SLICED

1 KG (2 LB) QUINCES, HALVED OR QUARTERED,
DESEEDED, BUT NOT PEELED

SALT

1 TEASPOON PEPPER

Cut the meat into large pieces and place in a pan with the oil, saffron and one-third of the onions. Cover with water and simmer with the lid on for 45 minutes, stirring occasionally. (The meat is cooked when it can be easily removed from the bone with a fork.) Remove the meat from the pan and set aside.

Keep the pan on the heat and add the quinces, the remaining onion and a little salt and pepper.

Add water to reach halfway up the pan's contents, mix well and reduce over medium heat to form a rich, thick sauce. Check how the quinces are progressing as some will cook more rapidly than others. Partially remove the pan from the heat and set aside the quinces as they become tender. When they are all cooked through return them to the pan, together with the meat, and reheat over medium heat.

Serve the meat on a plate, smothered with the quince sauce.

Kefta (meatballs) tagine

SERVES 4
PREPARATION TIME: 25 MINUTES
COOKING TIME: 25 MINUTES

FOR THE KEFTA (MEATBALLS):
½ ONION, GRATED
½ BUNCH OF CORIANDER (CILANTRO), CHOPPED
4 SPRIGS FRESH MINT, CHOPPED
500 G (4 CUPS) MINCED (GROUND) MEAT (PREFERABLY BEEF)
1 TEASPOON MILD CHILLI POWDER
1 TEASPOON GROUND CUMIN, PLUS EXTRA TO GARNISH
½ TEASPOON GROUND CINNAMON
1 TABLESPOON OIL
SALT

FOR THE SAUCE:
4 TOMATOES, SKINNED (SEE PAGE 34)
2 TABLESPOONS OIL
½ ONION, THINLY SLICED
SALT
1 TEASPOON GROUND CUMIN
PINCH OF SAFFRON
½ TEASPOON MILD CHILLI POWDER

To prepare the meatballs: Mix together the onion, coriander (cilantro) and mint. Add the meat, spices, oil and a little salt and mix well with just enough water to combine the mixture. Form the mixture into balls about the size of billiard balls.

To prepare the sauce: Dice the tomatoes. Heat the oil in a pan and add the onions, tomatoes and salt. Add the cumin, saffron and chilli powder and moisten with a little hot water. Stir, cover and continue cooking for a further 15 minutes to create a sauce, adding more hot water if necessary.

Add the meatballs to the sauce and simmer until they are cooked through, stirring occasionally.

Remove the meatballs from the sauce to prevent them from disintegrating and keep warm. Reduce the sauce if necessary. Serve the meatballs, covered with the sauce and dusted with ground cumin.

Serving suggestions:

This tagine is frequently served with eggs, cracked one at a time into the sauce, and cooked for a few minutes until cooked through.

Kefta brochettes

SERVES 4
PREPARATION TIME: 20 MINUTES
COOKING TIME: 10 MINUTES

500 G (4 CUPS) MINCED (GROUND) MEAT
½ ONION, GRATED
1 TABLESPOON CHOPPED
CORIANDER (CILANTRO)
½ TABLESPOON CHOPPED PARSLEY
½ TEASPOON GROUND CINNAMON
½ TEASPOON MILD CHILLI POWDER
½ TABLESPOON GROUNDNUT (PEANUT) OIL
1 TABLESPOON COLD WATER
SALT
½ TEASPOON GROUND PEPPER
½ TEASPOON GROUND CUMIN

Combine the meat, onion, coriander (cilantro), parsley, cinnamon, chilli powder and oil. Add the water, season with salt and pepper, then form the mixture into small oval shapes and thread on metal skewers. Cook the brochettes on the barbecue or under a hot grill (broiler). Serve dusted with ground cumin.

Alternative method:

You could also make small oval shapes and cook them in a pan with a mixture of butter, oil and pepper. This method results in a much smoother texture.

LEFT
Kefta is an Arab term that simply means minced (ground) meat. Kefta can be made from one type of meat or a mixture of different meats.

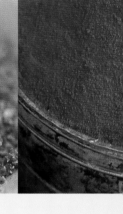

Sudanese felfel, hot chilli pepper, should be used sparingly and should never be placed directly on the tongue.

The term Nouioura refers to ground small mild chillies from Jamaica used at the end of cooking to add aroma to soups and vegetable tagines.

A mild dark red powder, ground from red (bell) peppers, paprika is highly prized in Morocco.

Fresh mild chillies, felfel hlou are eaten as soon as they are cooked.

Aromatic chillies, such as felfel har, contain a substance called capsaicin, a chemical irritant which is present in concentrated form in spicy dishes, and should therefore be consumed in moderation.

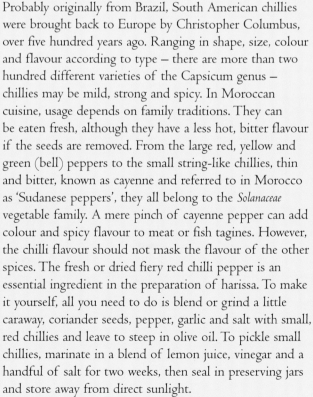

Harissa, the hot chilli, caraway, coriander, garlic and olive oil-based sauce, is more characteristic of Tunisian cuisine.

Various chillies, including this one from Jamaica, go into the complex combination of 27 spices used to make ras-el-hanout.

CHILLI PEPPERS

Probably originally from Brazil, South American chillies were brought back to Europe by Christopher Columbus, over five hundred years ago. Ranging in shape, size, colour and flavour according to type – there are more than two hundred different varieties of the Capsicum genus – chillies may be mild, strong and spicy. In Moroccan cuisine, usage depends on family traditions. They can be eaten fresh, although they have a less hot, bitter flavour if the seeds are removed. From the large red, yellow and green (bell) peppers to the small string-like chillies, thin and bitter, known as cayenne and referred to in Morocco as 'Sudanese peppers', they all belong to the *Solanaceae* vegetable family. A mere pinch of cayenne pepper can add colour and spicy flavour to meat or fish tagines. However, the chilli flavour should not mask the flavour of the other spices. The fresh or dried fiery red chilli pepper is an essential ingredient in the preparation of harissa. To make it yourself, all you need to do is blend or grind a little caraway, coriander seeds, pepper, garlic and salt with small, red chillies and leave to steep in olive oil. To pickle small chillies, marinate in a blend of lemon juice, vinegar and a handful of salt for two weeks, then seal in preserving jars and store away from direct sunlight.

Chicken tagine with olives and lemons

SERVES 6

PREPARATION TIME: 30 MINUTES

COOKING TIME: 1 HOUR

2 MEDIUM-SIZE FREE-RANGE CHICKENS

2 LARGE ONIONS, CHOPPED

1 BUNCH OF CORIANDER (CILANTRO),
FINELY CHOPPED

½ BUNCH OF FLAT-LEAF PARSLEY,
FINELY CHOPPED

2 CLOVES GARLIC, CRUSHED

4 TABLESPOONS OLIVE OIL

1 TEASPOON GROUND CUMIN

1 TEASPOON MILD CHILLI POWDER

1 SACHET (ENVELOPE) GROUND SAFFRON

SALT

1 TEASPOON GROUND WHITE PEPPER

6 PRESERVED LEMONS

36 OLIVES

Lemons preserved in brine can be bought, ready-made, from Middle Eastern delicatessens, or can be made at home (see page 66).

The olives used in this tagine have purplish coloured skins and a slightly bitter flavour.

Cut the chickens into pieces. Combine the onions, coriander (cilantro), parsley, and garlic in a heavy pan; add the oil, ½ teaspoon of the ground cumin, the chilli powder, saffron and about 400 ml (1¾ cups) water. Season with salt and pepper and mix well. Finally, add the chicken, making sure that the pieces are thoroughly coated with the sauce.

Cover and bring to the boil. Turn the chicken, reduce the heat to medium and cook for 25 minutes.

Reduce the heat to low and continue cooking for 15 minutes, checking at regular intervals.

As soon as the meat begins to fall off the bones, remove the chicken from the pan. Preheat the oven to 220°C (425°F), Gas Mark 7.

Place the chicken in an ovenproof dish; spread with some of the sauce and cook in the oven for about 10 minutes or until golden brown.

Meanwhile, reduce the rest of the sauce along with the remaining ½ teaspoon of cumin, the preserved lemons and olives. Serve the chicken covered with the sauce.

Preserved lemons

FOR 12 LEMONS
PREPARATION TIME: 20 MINUTES
STANDING TIME: 3 WEEKS
KEEP FOR: 3 MONTHS

1 KG (2 LB) UNWAXED THIN-SKINNED LEMONS
4 TABLESPOONS COARSE SALT
4 TABLESPOONS LEMON JUICE
WATER

Scrub the whole lemons under running water and place in a large bowl.
Cover with cold water and leave the lemons to soak for 3 days.
Strain the fruit and with a sharp-pointed knife slice the lemons lengthways without cutting right through so that the segments remain joined at one end.
Quickly scald a glass preserving jar and turn it upside down to drain completely.

Ease open the individual segments of each lemon and, with a spoon, fill the gaps between the segments with 3 tablespoons of the coarse salt. Pack the lemons tightly into the preserving jar in layers, as you go along, with the open ends upwards to prevent the salt from sinking to the bottom. Pour in the remaining tablespoon of coarse salt and the lemon juice.
Fill the preserving jar with boiling water. Press the lemons down with a heavy object to make sure that they are fully submerged. Seal the jar.
These preserved lemons will be ready to eat in 3 weeks' time and will keep for a further 3 months. You could use the juice on its own to replace vinegar in salads, and the peel to add flavour to tagines and other simmered dishes.

Green (bell) peppers in brine

FOR 12 (BELL) PEPPERS
PREPARATION TIME: 10 MINUTES
STANDING TIME: 2 WEEKS
KEEP FOR: 3 MONTHS

12 GREEN (BELL) PEPPERS
WATER
500 G (3 CUPS) COARSE SALT

Remove the stalks from the (bell) peppers.

Place the (bell) peppers in a previously scalded preserving jar and cover them with water containing the coarse salt.

Seal the preserving jar. Turn upside down, leave for a few hours, then turn the jar the right way up.

These (bell) peppers will be ready to eat in 2 weeks' time and can be used in salads or vegetable tagines.

Use the same recipe and method to preserve crushed green olives instead of (bell) peppers.

ABOVE

Female company and gossip is part of the delight of cooking for festive occasions, when numerous painstaking and complex preparations involve hours of work.

Chebbakiya
(honey cake or Ramadan cake)

MAKES 30
PREPARATION TIME: 60 MINUTES (INCLUDING 15 MINUTES STANDING TIME)
COOKING TIME: 5 MINUTES EACH

1 KG (8 CUPS) PLAIN (ALL-PURPOSE) FLOUR
300 G (1¼ CUPS) SESAME SEEDS
150 G (⅔ CUP) GROUND ANISEED
150 G (⅔ CUP) BUTTER
PINCH OF SALT
1 EGG
2 TABLESPOONS WHITE WINE VINEGAR
15 G (½ OZ) YEAST
PINCH OF SUGAR
1 TEASPOON GROUND CINNAMON
PINCH OF SAFFRON
200 ML (SCANT 1 CUP) ORANGE-FLOWER WATER
OIL FOR FRYING
2 KG (8 CUPS) CLEAR HONEY
PINCH OF GUM ARABIC

The succulent twists of fried golden pastry, honey-flavoured and sprinkled with sesame seeds, are consumed after sundown throughout the month of Ramadan. In certain regions, they are also known as griouches.

Stir together the flour, half the sesame seeds and the aniseed; add the butter, salt, egg, vinegar, and the yeast diluted in 100 ml (scant ½ cup) lukewarm water with a pinch of sugar. Mix in the cinnamon, saffron and sufficient orange-flower water to make a dough. Knead well for 15 minutes.

Divide the pastry into balls the size of a small tangerine. Cover with a tea towel (dishcloth) and leave to rise for 15 minutes. Flatten the balls to a thickness of about 1.5 cm (¾ inch) and cut into 10 x 5-cm (4 x 2-in) rectangles. Cut each rectangle into 4 strips, keeping one end of the rectangle intact. To shape into a cake, plait (braid) the individual strips, then pinch the ends together. Finally, firmly join both ends of the plait (braid) together to form a circle. Place the cake on an ungreased surface. Repeat for the remaining cakes.

Heat about 2.5 cm (1 inch) of oil in a pan. Place the cakes carefully in the heated oil, without crushing them. Turn the cakes to make sure that they are golden brown on both sides. Remove with a slotted spoon and drain on kitchen paper (paper towels). Meanwhile, bring the honey, any remaining orange-flower water and the gum arabic to the boil in a deep pan. Drop the chebbakiya into the honey, then remove with a slotted spoon, drain again and sprinkle with the rest of the sesame seeds.

Sugared and salted, rghaïfs aren't easy to make and require premium quality flour. With a little practice and dexterity, however, these delicate smooth pancakes made from dough that has been folded several times, make a delightful breakfast treat.

Rghaïfs (pancakes)

MAKES 20
PREPARATION TIME: 30 MINUTES
STANDING TIME 10 MINUTES
COOKING TIME: 10 MINUTES EACH

1 TEASPOON YEAST
1 KG (8 CUPS) PLAIN (ALL-PURPOSE)
FLOUR, SIFTED
1 TABLESPOON OIL
1 TEASPOON SALT
500 ML (GENEROUS 2 CUPS) OIL FOR FRYING
TO DECORATE:
HONEY
ICING (CONFECTIONERS') SUGAR

Blend the yeast with 4 tablespoons lukewarm water in a bowl. On a work surface (counter), knead the flour, yeast liquid, 1 tablespoon oil, 250 ml (1 cup) lukewarm water and the salt to form a smooth, elastic dough (similar to bread dough). Coat your hands in oil and shape the dough into egg-size balls, then leave to rise for 10 minutes.

Oil your hands again and pick up a ball of dough. Place on an oiled surface and stretch the dough lengthways and sideways with your fingertips, to form a thin sheet of dough, the thickness of a pancake. Fold the sides of the sheet into the middle to form a rectangle. Then fold in both ends of the rectangle to make a square. Repeat the procedure with the remaining balls. Flatten the squares, one by one, and fry in the oil, until golden brown.

Serve with honey or a little icing (confectioners') sugar.

Note: Alternatively, *rghaifs* can be cooked on an oiled griddle or in a heavy, non-stick frying pan (skillet). *Rghaifs* may be stuffed with meat or vegetables, as a savoury dish; or with chopped toasted almonds as a sweet version.

SOFT DRINKS المشروبات الطيبة

Morocco offers a selection of succulent fruits. Its soft, sweet oranges yield excellent juice, enhanced by a soupçon of cinnamon to bring out the flavour. Pomegranate juice, fresh grape juice or juice produced from dried fruit can be combined with sugar, lemon juice and a little orange-flower water. As for cherry juice, this is a speciality of the Sefrou region, where fine cherry trees abound. Milk from cows, sheep or camels quenches the thirst and is drunk to break the fast in the evenings during Ramadan. As with dates, it is used to welcome official visitors, young brides or pilgrims upon their return from Mecca, as a token of hospitality. Almond milk is drunk on festive occasions. Once they are delicately peeled, blanched almonds form a smooth paste to which sugar is added. Banana milk, milk flavoured with sweet marjoram or orange flowers, or simply *lben*, whey, which has a sour and refreshing taste, is served as an accompaniment for couscous; these traditional drinks certainly compete, in the popularity stakes with lemonade and Coca-Cola. At table, water is not offered directly but instead is placed on a tray nearby. In general, water is drunk only at the end of a meal. At certain times of the day tea, the national drink, is replaced by *cassé*, a strong coffee served black or with a dash of milk if preferred. Prepared according to secret recipes, coffee is sometimes flavoured with cinnamon, orange-flower water and spices – aniseed, cardamom, ginger and nutmeg.

Made from finely chopped blanched almonds, water and milk, almond milk is a festive drink.

In middle-class households, coffee for special occasions is supplemented with spices that are left to infuse, or simply with whole peppercorns.

Arranged in a pyramid shape on pushcarts or on market stalls, Marrakech or Beni Mellal oranges are the most widely renowned for their juiciness and flavour.

This attractively decorated glass contains milk flavoured with orange-flower water.

Sugared (sugared couscous with raisins) (seffa)

SERVES 6–8
PREPARATION TIME: 15 MINUTES
COOKING TIME: 30 MINUTES

625 G (3⅓ CUPS) MEDIUM OR FINE
GROUND COUSCOUS
150 G (1 CUP) RAISINS
CASTER (SUPERFINE) SUGAR

TO DECORATE:
100 G (SCANT 1 CUP) ICING
(CONFECTIONERS') SUGAR
1 TABLESPOON GROUND CINNAMON
A FEW ALMONDS AND DATES (OPTIONAL)

Cook the couscous according to the standard recipe (see page 150).
Rinse the raisins thoroughly and drain. Just before the couscous is cooked place the raisins in the bottom section of the couscousiere or steamer and replace the top section containing the couscous.
When these ingredients are cooked, add a little sugar to the raisins and mix well with the couscous.
Draw the couscous up into a dome shape on a serving dish.
Decorate the top with alternate stripes of the sugar and cinnamon, using a small sieve, and sprinkle a few almonds or dates around the edge, if you like.
Serve hot, accompanied by mint tea or milk.

Miel de la mariée (Bride's honey)

SERVES 20
PREPARATION TIME: 20 MINUTES
COOKING TIME: 15 MINUTES

1 KG HONEY
1 TEASPOON GROUND DRIED ROSEBUDS
1 TEASPOON CINNAMON POWDER
¼ TEASPOON GROUND PEPPER
¼ TEASPOON GROUND CLOVES
PINCH OF SAFFRON
PINCH OF GROUND GUM ARABIC

Stir all the ingredients in a pan and allow to infuse without letting it come to the boil. If possible use a double boiler or a bowl set over a pan of simmering water. Pour into a *taous* (earthenware serving bowl) leave to cool and decorate with blanched and toasted chopped almonds and a few sesame seeds.
This recipe is prepared for occasions such as engagements, weddings, or circumcisions.

LEFT
The charm of seffa, with its generously buttered and steamed fine grains, lies in its decorative presentation that alternates thin strands of cinnamon with sugar.

المزواج MARRIAGE TRADITIONS

Symbols of purity and prosperity, milk, honey, dates, loaf sugar, rosewater or orange-flower water are all inextricably linked with the celebration of marriage. The bride's feet are washed in milk, and the mother of the groom welcomes her new daughter-in-law with milk and dates. An egg, cracked open on the threshold of the newlyweds' home represents a token of fertility. The same applies to the silver fish, a ubiquitous symbol at wedding ceremonies. It is also a tradition in Fès that the young bride prepares a fish tagine for their first breakfast, on the day after the wedding. To affirm her new life, in the bosom of her in-laws, she bakes a loaf of bread, as a symbol of abundance in her new family home. Sugar represents good luck. In rural areas women, bearing 2-kg (4-lb) cones of loaf sugar wrapped in thick mauve-coloured paper, offer them as a token of happiness to the young bride. The ritual of exchanging gifts between the families is equally important. Rich fabrics, elaborate slippers, loaf sugar, oil, jewels and perfumes are offered to the bride by her future husband. A breakfast, presented by the bride's mother, is dedicated to the couple's first day of married life. On the menu: *sfenj* (orange doughnuts), rice cooked in milk, steamed lamb's head and sweetmeats.

RIGHT
The evocatively termed, Gazelle's Horns are sometimes also compared to the crescent of the moon. These horn-shaped pastries will remain fresh for up to 10 days, if kept in an airtight container.

Gazelle's horns

MAKES 70
PREPARATION TIME: 2 HOURS
STANDING TIME: 30 MINUTES, PLUS OVERNIGHT
COOKING TIME: 30 MINUTES

FOR THE FILLING:

1 KG (8 CUPS) BLANCHED ALMONDS

750 G (SCANT 3½ CUPS) CASTER (SUPERFINE) SUGAR

300 G (1¼ CUPS) CLARIFIED BUTTER

1 TEASPOON ORANGE-FLOWER WATER

½ TEASPOON ALMOND ESSENCE (EXTRACT)

1 TEASPOON GROUND GUM ARABIC

SALT

FOR THE PASTRY:

500 G (4 CUPS) PLAIN (ALL-PURPOSE) FLOUR

1 TABLESPOON CLARIFIED BUTTER

200 ML (SCANT 1 CUP) ORANGE-FLOWER WATER

SALT

To prepare the filling: Blend the almonds and sugar in a food processor or pass through a mincing (grinding) machine. Add the butter (preferably warm and frothy), orange-flower water, almond essence (extract), gum arabic and a pinch of salt and knead by hand to form a smooth stiff paste, but loose enough to handle.

To prepare the pastry: Mix all the ingredients together, adding the liquid gradually as it may not all be needed, and form into a large ball. Divide into smaller walnut-size balls, put in a bowl, cover with clingfilm (plastic wrap) and leave to stand for 30 minutes.

Roll out the pastry balls into thin pliable rounds about 5–6 cm (2–2½ inches) in diameter.

Place a cigar-shaped piece of almond filling on one half of each round. Dampen the edges, fold over the other half and seal firmly.

Carefully bend the pastries into horn or crescent shapes and trim the excess pastry with a pastry cutter.

Chill overnight in the refrigerator.

Preheat the oven to 140°C (275°F), Gas Mark 1.

With a knitting needle, pierce 3 holes on each side of the horns, to prevent them from splitting during baking.

Place on baking trays and bake for about 30 minutes until lightly coloured.

Orange and cinnamon salad

SERVES 4

PREPARATION: 25 MINUTES

6 LARGE ORANGES PLUS JUICE OF 1 EXTRA ORANGE

2 TABLESPOONS ORANGE-FLOWER WATER

2 TABLESPOONS CASTER (SUPERFINE) SUGAR

2 CINNAMON STICKS

1 TEASPOON GROUND CINNAMON

1 TEASPOON ICING (CONFECTIONERS') SUGAR

4 SPRIGS MINT, TO DECORATE

Place the juice of 1 orange, the orange-flower water, caster (superfine) sugar and cinnamon sticks in a pan. Bring to the boil and continue to boil for 5 minutes. Leave to cool, then discard the cinnamon. With a sharp knife slice off the peel and all the white pith from the oranges and cut them into rounds. Arrange in small bowls and pour the cooled syrup over them.
Serve dusted with icing (confectioners') sugar and decorated with the mint sprigs.

ORANGES

Oranges enhance Moroccan cooking and accompany numerous sweet dishes, as well as savoury ones, such as chicken tagine with caramelized oranges.

During their numerous visits to Morocco, at the beginning of the twentieth century, the brothers Tharaud wrote: 'You find yourself here, pausing amid the fabulous Atlas Mountains. These oranges that you pick so casually, without fearing the appearance of the dragon with a hundred heads, are indeed the famous golden apples of the garden of the Hesperides.' Arranged in sumptuous pyramid displays on pushcarts or stalls in the souks, Moroccan oranges are bursting with juice and sunshine. In gardens or along the avenues of Marrakech, orange trees in full flower fill the air with their sweet fragrance. The Greeks first discovered the orange tree in Morocco and then transplanted it elsewhere throughout the Mediterranean. In Agadir's hinterland, orange-tree plantations flourish side by side across the flat open countryside of Sous and extend as far as the slopes of the High Atlas Mountains in the north and to the slopes of the Anti-Atlas Mountains in the south. No less than five different types of oranges grow in their thousands, ripening in close succession. Exported worldwide, navel oranges are ready from November onwards, then sanguinettis (blood oranges) and finally the varieties with the finest reputation, the bitter-flavoured, slightly acidic bigarade oranges. Oranges are associated with a number of dishes, often dredged with cinnamon, and are also a key ingredient in many savoury, sweet-and-sour recipes.

الشاي بالنعناع MINT TEA

From Fès to Rabat, or in nomads' tents, served at any hour of the day, mint tea unites men sitting on café terraces or women at the *hammam* (Turkish bath), or is used to clinch a business transaction or to welcome a visitor. The tea ritual requires two trays. One tray holds the small straight glasses made of Saint-Louis crystal or simple glassware and the traditional electro-plated teapot with a long spout and pointed lid. The other tray holds silver boxes containing sugar, green tea and fresh mint. The water is boiled in a copper samovar. Into the scalded and rinsed teapot, the host places tea leaves, the neatly tied bunch of mint and large chunks of sugar, before pouring on the boiling water and allowing the tea to steep. Poured into a glass and poured back into the teapot several times to make sure that it is well blended, then sampled, the tea will not be offered to guests until the host considers it to be perfect. Only then, with a flowing and precise gesture, will the host raise the teapot on high above the glasses and commence pouring the aromatic tea, in long, piping-hot streams. Marjoram, aniseed, saffron, rosemary or orange-flower water may be added to complete the subtle flavour of mint tea.

Tea is prepared in the presence of guests. The number of tea glasses always outnumbers the guests present.

Perfect tea depends on the quality of the green tea and the fresh mint, where whole bunches of the fragrant leaves are steeped in the teapot.

The 2-kg (4-lb) cones of loaf sugar, wrapped in thick mauve-coloured paper, are broken into pieces using a small copper or wooden hammer.

Large chunks of sugar are arranged on top of the mint to prevent the leaves from rising to the surface.

Coastal regions of
Morocco

السواحل المغربية

From the Algerian border to the Mediterranean border, the sandy beaches and countless fishing ports of Morocco cover roughly 3,500 km (2,175 miles) of coastline. Since time immemorial the Atlantic and Mediterranean coastal regions have been exposed to the influence of the outside world through traders and conquerors leaving their mark. The Phoenicians were the first to

LEFT

Small pieces of multicoloured glazed earthenware, zelliges, are chiselled to form a mosaic pattern and then arranged according to very strict rules of colour sequence.

RIGHT

Carrying sacks of grain and large water bottles or produce from the souks in its straw panniers, the donkey in Morocco is the essential companion on all journeys.

reach the coasts of Morocco, some 30 centuries ago. They set up trading posts at Lixus (Liks), Salé, and on the Isle of Mogador. They bartered wine and spices for wool, animal hides and livestock. Then came the Romans. Beginning in the year 146 BC, they founded prosperous towns and transformed the north of Morocco into a huge wheat granary. A hundred or so fish salting operations and factories producing garum, an anchovy paste highly prized by the Romans, were set up in Lixus. Made from fish entrails, the strong-smelling paste was left to steep in salt and then used to season meat and vegetables. The fish were processed and covered in salt, in order to preserve them for their onward journey to Rome.

The Portuguese and Spanish have occupied the Atlantic coastal regions since the early fourteenth century. They set up trading outposts along the Saharan gold trail. From Tangier to Agadir, the city walls of Asilah, the citadel of Azzemour, the city of El Jadida or Essaouira (formerly Mogador), all bear testimony to the former trading activities of the Portuguese who would buy jellabas (full-length cotton tunics), wheat, or horses and exchange them for slaves and gold in black Africa.

The last Muslims to be expelled from Spain at the beginning of the seventeenth century settled in the coastal towns – Rabat, where the naval war broke out with the Christian Spaniards, sheltered around three thousand refugee families. In these towns, Jewish refugees, Christian mercenaries, Moors, European adventurers, all rubbed shoulders in the midst of Arab and Berber populations. The Portuguese and Spanish held sway until the end of the sixteenth century. The Spanish, who controlled the north of the country for many years, still retain jurisdiction over two enclosed cities, the praesidia of Ceuta and Melilla.

The arrival of new products via the various ports was largely responsible for the way in which Moroccan culinary traditions have evolved over the years. Although green tea seems to have been part and parcel of everyday life in Morocco since the beginning of time, it was only introduced as recently as 1854, during the Crimean War. Denied access to Slav countries, because of the blockade across the Baltic, English traders turned their attentions to seeking out new commercial opportunities elsewhere, channelling their merchandise through the trading ports of Tangier and Mogador instead. Since then, the people of Morocco have quenched their thirst with infusions of green tea blended with two dominant flavours: mint and absinthe.

Inevitably, the characteristic cuisine that developed throughout the coastal regions of Morocco was heavily influenced by the abundant natural resources of both seas. A centre for the country's large- and small-scale fishing industry, Moroccan waters are among the most densely populated with fish in the world. Neither fishermen nor seafarers by tradition, the people of Morocco have nevertheless succeeded in allowing modern fishing techniques coexist with traditional methods to match local supply and demand.

Consequently, fresh fish is, by choice, a staple food of the nation. Wooden boats moored in the ports of Safi, Essaouira, Agadir or Tan Tan – trawlers, sardine boats or small motorboats – are dedicated to sardine, mackerel or anchovy fishing. In the past sardines used to be preserved in brine. Nowadays they are marinated, fresh, in *chermoula* (a cumin, crushed garlic and coriander [cilantro], mild chilli and lemon based sauce) and covered in olive oil. Today, Safi canned sardines are world famous. Freshwater shads, whiting, sar, sea bream, pageots (also called 'daurade rose', pink sea bream) and Mediterranean grouper, bass and mullet are among the most frequently eaten fish in Morocco. Cooked in the oven, in a tagine, fried or mixed with tomatoes, all types of fish are usually marinated in chermoula: fish pastilla, sardines stuffed with spices, fish briouat, fish kefta, fish filled with dates and almonds, fish marinated or stuffed with walnuts… the range of fish recipes is endless. Fish dishes are marinated with spices according to type and each coastal region has its own unique way of preparing fish. Freshwater shad is enjoyed for its oily skin and the female roe. Fish couscous is served mainly in the regions of Safi, Agadir and Salé. It is tricky to prepare and should only be made from the freshest of fish that will remain firm during cooking. The bouillon is always passed through a strainer to prevent an unfortunate accident with a fish bone! Fish dishes are not allowed to escape the sweet-and-sour culinary treatment so dear to the Moroccan palate! Conger eel couscous with onions, raisins, cinnamon and honey is a Rabat speciality.

LEFT
This ancient Andalusian palace in El Jadida was constructed in 1497 and restored in 1980 and has since been converted into a hotel. The stucco, intricate white sculptured plasterwork, produced using stencils and a compass, is an essential part of the décor of all prestigious edifices, adorning walls, archways and door frames.

A sweet-and-sour dish of fish with almonds, coated in breadcrumbs is a firm favourite with the local population of Safi. Cornmeal replaces wheat in *baddaz*, couscous with conger eel. Sun-dried mussels are a special treat in couscous dishes. Crunchy fried fish rolled in egg and breadcrumbs then coated with semolina are extremely popular. At Essaouira, just a short distance away from

FROM LEFT TO RIGHT

Built on a rock, a stone's throw from Casablanca, the small village of Sidi Abderrahman defies the ocean at high tide, as indeed do the fishermen who cast their lines into the restless waves of the Atlantic Ocean.

the blue-painted fishing trawlers where seagulls hover expectantly overhead, sardines, sole, mackerel or squid, grilled (broiled) on the quayside, may be sampled fresh off the boats.

In certain coastal areas, it is customary to eat fish 'au gratin', with boiled eggs, spiced with saffron, onions and preserved lemons. Oualidya stakes its reputation on the oysters that are bred in the lagoon of this small seaside town. Superb shellfish, such as cockles and mussels, as well as king prawns (jumbo shrimp) and sea urchins can also be enjoyed in Oualidya. South of Tan Tan, sparkling grey cliffs, some 40 metres (130 feet) above the ocean, hug the jagged, eroded coastline. Overhanging the edge of the drop, fishermen perch precariously, day-in, day-out, hoping to catch a few sea bass, sea bream or occasionally courbines (bass-perch). Using reels and lines with sardines as bait, they struggle to haul in the fish,

risking life and limb, simply to sell their catch down at the port in Tan Tan.

Market gardeners and fruit sellers are very much in evidence throughout the rich, fertile open lands of Sous that stretch between Agadir and Taroudannt. Oranges, lemons and melons are piled high in the shade of the cypress and yew tree hedges. Under Saadian rule, sugar cane plantations necessitated the installation of extensive irrigation networks. These constructions were destroyed at the beginning of the seventeenth century but it meant, nevertheless, that the sultan was in a position to exchange sugar for tons of Italian marble. Also in the open country-side of Sous, in the region around Agadir, from Safi right up to the foothills of the Anti-Atlas mountain range, vast expanses of delicious oil-producing arganier trees reign supreme. In these wild, arid regions the trunks and spiked branches of these trees stand proud against the heat and arid desert conditions. The arganier grows exclusively in Morocco and thrives in certain areas on steeply inclined terrain where its root system is deeply embedded in the soil. The oil is extracted from the kernels of the fruit, which resembles huge yellowish olives. At one time the extraction was the work of women, through a tedious process of kneading and pressing. This produced only enough oil for local consumption, but modern growing and production methods have created an export market. Used hot or cold, argan oil adds a delightful aroma to fish and egg dishes. It is also one the main ingredients of *amlou*, a dessert famous throughout Sous. Made from ground and lightly toasted almonds, honey and argan oil, this blend will keep for up to two months. *Amlou* is traditionally offered to young married couples on their wedding night.

LEFT
A traditional Rabat house, with its studded wooden door and cobbled floor.

ABOVE
The fishing boats in the shipbuilding yards of Essaouira are still made entirely of wood, using age-old traditional construction techniques.

The windswept Atlantic coast offers superb panoramic views over the ocean, particularly along the stretch between Essaouira and Agadir. Ancient whitewashed Portuguese-style villages punctuate the long sandy beaches, the natural lagoons attract migratory birds, and in the fishing ports seagulls, with their ear-piercing cries, hover overhead. At Essaouira, some of the women still wear long sweeping white robes that cover them from head to toe.

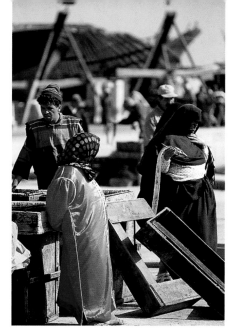

Fish briouats

MAKES 8
PREPARATION TIME: 30 MINUTES
COOKING TIME: 5 MINUTES EACH

1 TEASPOON OLIVE OIL
125 G (4 OZ) FRESH COD, CHOPPED
50 G (2 OZ) PRAWNS (SHRIMP), COOKED
AND PEELED
2 CLOVES GARLIC, CRUSHED
½ TEASPOON CORIANDER (CILANTRO),
COARSELY CHOPPED
1 TEASPOON PARSLEY, COARSELY CHOPPED
¼ TEASPOON GROUND CUMIN
4 SHEETS FILO PASTRY (8 SHEETS BRIK)
OIL FOR FRYING
LEMON SLICES

Heat the olive oil in a large, heavy pan
and lightly brown all the ingredients,
stirring gently.

Cut 2 rounds (20-cm/8-inch diameter)
from each filo sheet and fold in half.
Place a portion of the fish mixture on
each semi-circle, fold over into a
quadrant and seal the edges firmly. Heat
the frying oil in a pan and fry the
briouats until golden brown.

Drain on kitchen paper (paper towels)
and serve hot with lemon slices.

Fish pastilla

SERVES 8
PREPARATION TIME: 30 MINUTES
COOKING TIME: 1 HOUR

1 KG (2 LB) SQUID
3 TABLESPOONS GROUNDNUT (PEANUT) OIL
1 KG (2 LB) PRAWNS (SHRIMP), PEELED
2 CLOVES GARLIC, SLICED
4 TABLESPOONS LEMON JUICE
SALT, PEPPER
1 LARGE FILLET OF HADDOCK OR COD
1 ONION, SLICED
1 LARGE BUNCH OF PARSLEY, CHOPPED
1 LARGE BUNCH OF CORIANDER
(CILANTRO), CHOPPED
6 SHEETS FILO PASTRY (10 SHEETS BRIK)
1 EGG YOLK

Rinse the squid, pat dry and cut into small
pieces. Heat the oil in a deep pan; brown the
squid and prawns (shrimp) in the hot oil
with the garlic, lemon juice and a little salt
and pepper for about 10 minutes.

Meanwhile, simmer the fish in water over
medium heat for 10 minutes, with the
onion, parsley, coriander (cilantro) and a
little salt and pepper.

Remove from the pan and drain. Flake
the fish and add to the squid and prawns
(shrimp). Cook gently for 10 minutes.

Preheat the oven to 150°C (300°F), Gas
Mark 2.

Line a greased pie dish with 5 or 6 half-
sheets of pastry, allowing a generous overlap
around the rim. Place 1 whole sheet, folded
in half, in the centre to strengthen the pie
base. Spread the fish mixture on the pastry
base; fold over the edges, then cover with the
remaining pastry sheets, tucking in under
the edges. Seal with the egg yolk, using a
pastry brush.

Bake in the oven for 35 minutes.

Serve hot.

Chorba

SERVES 8

PREPARATION TIME: 30 MINUTES

COOKING TIME: 1 HOUR

Chorba, a light style harira (see page 40), is made from the stock of steamed meats. This soup is not thickened with flour.

Ingredients may include:

DICED STEAMED RED MEAT

DICED STEAMED CHICKEN

DICED VEGETABLES, SUCH AS COURGETTES (ZUCCHINI), CARROTS, TURNIPS, POTATOES

CHOPPED CORIANDER (CILANTRO)

2 CHOPPED TOMATOES

125–175 G (4–6 OZ) VERMICELLI

SAFFRON, SALT AND PEPPER

Bouillon de l'accouchée
(New mother's broth)

SERVES 1

PREPARATION TIME: 15 MINUTES

COOKING TIME: 1 HOUR

4 CLOVES GARLIC

2 LARGE ONIONS

1 CHICKEN

1 BUNCH PARSLEY, CHOPPED

1 TABLESPOON RAS-EL-HANOUT

1 TEASPOON THYME LEAVES

1 TEASPOON PEPPERMINT, CHOPPED

1 TEASPOON GROUND PEPPER

Chop the garlic and onions, then set the onions aside.

Stuff the chicken with all the other ingredients.

Bring 2 litres (8 cups) of water to the boil in a large pan. When the water reaches boiling point, add the chicken and the onions, lower the heat and simmer for about 1 hour.

When the chicken is cooked through, strain off the bouillon.

ABOVE

Chorba is often served with an accompaniment of dates or dried figs.

ﺍﻟﻤﻮﻟﺪ BIRTH CELEBRATIONS

Every celebration has its own particular form of gastronomic tradition. First and foremost childbirth is met with *youyous* (chant-like refrains) and chanting. In order to restore the energies of the young mother, a chicken bouillon is prepared, fortified with chopped garlic, saffron, thyme and wild mint, and served with raw eggs. Similarly, *sellou*, a cone made of flour and ground almonds, is reputed to have nutritional value and according to tradition is recommended to help the new mother's milk flow. The whole family takes part in bringing large baskets containing cakes, sugar, tea and even poultry, if it is a home birth, for the new mother. These offerings are kept for the big celebration that takes place on the seventh day following the birth. On that morning, all types of pancakes — *rghaif, mlaoui, beghrir* — are served and then a sheep is slaughtered to the accompaniment of the *shahada*, a Muslim prayer, and the business of choosing the child's forename, in the presence of all the family, takes place. In certain regions, it is customary to throw salt into all corners of the home to protect the baby from *jnoun*, evil spirits. A huge gathering of friends, family and neighbours at lunch or dinner is customary, when guests bring presents for the mother and new arrival.

ABOVE

A young mother who has just given birth is served this nourishing bouillon, accompanied by white chicken meat with stuffing and a raw egg, sprinkled with gum arabic.

ONION

MINT

GARLIC

CORIANDER
(CILANTRO)

GINGER

The indispensable onion is a basic ingredient for many dishes, as well as used as an accompaniment for salads.

Rarely used for cooking purposes, mint with its firm stalks and bright green leaves is synonymous with green tea and is always consumed fresh.

White or purple garlic is used to add flavour to dried vegetables, lentil and chickpea (garbanzo) based dishes.

Nicknamed 'Arabian parsley', coriander (cilantro), with its subtle flavour, is an essential ingredient in countless recipes.

Once peeled and grated, root ginger adds a piquant flavour to both sweet and savoury dishes.

FLAT LEAF
PARSLEY

الأعشاب الرطبة FRESH HERBS

Coriander (cilantro), parsley, mint, thyme, fennel, absinthe…
In the souks of Morocco, stalls of fresh herbs form a green curtain concealing their vendors. Most of these herbs are used fresh and will keep for several days, wrapped in a damp linen cloth, in the refrigerator. As well as their aroma, all these plants are renowned for their medicinal properties. Mint is synonymous with green tea and comes in about ten varieties. The fresh mint *naa-naa* is highly aromatic and is sold in bunches, whereas wild mint, like fennel, is used to add flavour to fish tagines. Coriander (cilantro), a delicate plant with white flowers, is used fresh and finely chopped. It is included in numerous recipes — soups, couscous bouillon, marinades, tagines… Flat leaf parsley — not the curly variety — is considered highly nutritional. Absinthe, a tall plant with silvery leaves, is cultivated in Morocco and is sometimes used as a substitute for mint in tea. It is known for stimulating the appetite. Thyme possesses countless beneficial properties including acting as a pick-me-up and an antiseptic. Broad leaf basil flourishes well in the sunny climate of Morocco. Sage and verbena, used for making infusions, rank high in aiding digestion. Garlic is a natural antiseptic. It is easier to digest if the central green shoot in each clove is removed before use. Onions are rich in sulphur, iodine, phosphorous and iron.

Flat leaf parsley is easy to grow. As with mint and coriander (cilantro), it is sold by the bunch on stalls in the souks, or by itinerant vendors.

Chermoula

Sardines stuffed with chermoula feature on all dinner tables the length and breadth of the Atlantic coastal region. In the open sea off Agadir, Safi and Essaouira, shoals of sardines migrate south during the summer season. Safi is renowned the world over for exporting canned sardines.

SERVES 6
PREPARATION TIME: 20 MINUTES
COOKING TIME: 5 MINUTES

2 LARGE CLOVES GARLIC
SALT
½ TEASPOON MILD CHILLI POWDER
½ TEASPOON GROUND CUMIN
¼ TEASPOON GROUND PEPPER
1 BUNCH OF CORIANDER (CILANTRO), CHOPPED
½ BUNCH OF FLAT LEAF PARSLEY, CHOPPED
4 TABLESPOONS LEMON JUICE
1 TEASPOON VINEGAR
1 TABLESPOON OIL

Grind the garlic, salt, chilli powder, cumin and pepper, using a pestle and mortar or a spice grinder, and reduce to a paste. Mix the ground spice paste with the herbs and blend with the lemon juice, vinegar and oil into a smooth paste. Heat all the ingredients in a pan over a gentle heat to release the aromas, but do not bring to the boil.
Chill before use.

This sauce can be used for both hot and cold dishes.

Sardines in chermoula

Serves 4
Preparation time: 30 minutes
Cooking time: 20 minutes

1 kg (2 lb) fresh sardines
Chermoula (see facing page)
plain (all-purpose) flour
oil for frying

Remove the sardine heads. Slit each fish lengthways, gut and remove the backbones. Rinse and flatten the sardines thoroughly with a mallet, then blot dry with kitchen paper (paper towels). Line the fish up in pairs and stuff with chermoula paste. Coat the stuffed sardines in flour and cook in hot oil for about 5 minutes on each side.

Fish brochettes

Serves 4
Preparation time: 20 minutes
Cooking time: 10 minutes

Fish (cod, monkfish, grouper)
cut into large dice
Chermoula (see facing page)
4 tomatoes
4 preserved lemons (see page 66)

Marinate the chunks of fish in the chermoula for several hours.
Thread the chunks of fish on to skewers, alternating with pieces of tomato and preserved lemon.
Place under a hot grill (broiler) or cook on a barbecue.
Serve with rice or tomato salad with mint (see page 140).

Fish tagine

SERVES 8

PREPARATION TIME: 20 MINUTES

COOKING TIME: 1½ HOURS

500 G (1 LB) TOMATOES
1 PRESERVED LEMON (SEE PAGE 66)
2 TABLESPOONS CHERMOULA (SEE PAGE 102)
4 TABLESPOONS OIL
½ TABLESPOON TOMATO PURÉE (PASTE)
1 SACHET (ENVELOPE) GROUND SAFFRON
8 THICK PORTIONS WHITE FISH
2 ONIONS, THINLY SLICED
2 GREEN (BELL) PEPPERS, THINLY SLICED

Preheat the oven to 150°C (300°F), Gas Mark 2.

Slice the tomatoes into rounds and the preserved lemon into slices lengthways.

Add 200 ml (scant 1 cup) water to the chermoula, then the oil, tomato purée (paste) and saffron and mix thoroughly. Divide and spread this mixture evenly over the individual portions of fish.

Cover the base of a deep, earthenware dish with a layer of half each of the onions, tomatoes and lemon slices. Cover with the fish, then with a layer of the remaining onions, tomatoes, lemon slices and the green (bell) peppers.

Cover with foil and cook in the oven for 1½ hours.

This recipe may also be cooked on the hob (stovetop). Midway through cooking, cover the pan and continue cooking for the final 45 minutes.

ABOVE

Medium-sized fish, of similar size to trout, can also be stuffed with chermoula and cooked whole, in a frying pan (skillet) or in the oven.

Fried alose (shad fish)

SERVES 8

PREPARATION TIME: 20 MINUTES

COOKING TIME: 5 MINUTES ON EACH SIDE

1 SHAD FISH (ABOUT 1 KG/2 LB), OR
8 MACKEREL OR HERRING
CHERMOULA (SEE PAGE 102)
5 TABLESPOONS PLAIN (ALL-PURPOSE) FLOUR
150 ML (⅔ CUP) OIL FOR FRYING

Scale and gut the shad (a fish with a very delicate skin, from the same family as herrings and sardines). Wash thoroughly and pat dry on kitchen paper (paper towels).

If using shad, cut into steaks about 2-cm (¾-inch) thick. Coat the shad steaks or the whole fish first in chermoula and then in the flour.

Heat the oil in a pan and fry the coated steaks or whole fish, turning them to make sure that they are browned evenly on both sides.

Leave to cool, then chill in the refrigerator. This dish is served cold.

Fish with saffron and onions

SERVES 6

PREPARATION TIME: 10 MINUTES

COOKING TIME: 30 MINUTES

2 KG (4 LB) FISH, SUCH AS SEA BREAM (PORGY),
PAGEOT (RED SEA BREAM) OR MULLET

6–8 TABLESPOONS GROUNDNUT (PEANUT) OIL

5 ONIONS, THINLY SLICED

1 TEASPOON GROUND GINGER

1–2 PINCHES OF SAFFRON

SALT

1–2 PRESERVED LEMONS, CUT INTO STRIPS
(SEE PAGE 66)

Preheat the oven to 160°C (325°F), Gas
Mark 3.

Cut the fish into large pieces and place in an
ovenproof dish or casserole, pour in the oil
and add the onions, ginger and saffron.
Cook in the oven for about 30 minutes or
until tender. If required, add a little water to
prevent the fish from sticking. Adjust the
seasoning and add the salt.

Add the lemon immediately before serving.
The sauce should not be too liquid. If
the sauce has not thickened sufficiently,
remove the fish and reduce the sauce over
high heat.

الزعفران

SAFFRON

The stigmas of the mauve-flowered
saffron crocus (*Crocus sativus*), are as
precious as gold dust.

Taliouine, between Ouarzazate and
Agadir, is where several hundred
hectares of saffron flowers grow at an
altitude of between 1,200 and 2,000
metres (4,000–6,500 feet) – on light,
chalky terrain. The bulbs are planted in
September and flower at the end of
October. The delicate procedure of
harvesting the crocus flowerheads lasts
between 15 and 20 days and should be
done before the flower heads open in
the sun. The red stigmas which, when
dried, become the precious saffron, are
then removed from the flower heads by
hand. Once the saffron has been dried
out it is placed, in waterproof sacks, out
of direct light to preserve its flavour.
It takes approximately 100,000 flowers
to produce 1 kg (2 lb) of saffron, and
one gram alone is sufficient to colour
7 litres (7½ quarts) of water. Top
quality saffron is in the form of whole
threads; the powdered version tends to
lose its flavour, very quickly. Saffron,
albeit expensive, is much sought after
for its incomparable taste, but turmeric
('the poor man's saffron') is often used
as a substitute in Moroccan cooking.

ABOVE
*Saffron powder, sold in
bulk in the markets, is
liable to deteriorate in
the open air or in
contact with other
perishables. Saffron
only retains its flavour,
as saffron threads,
when protected from
exposure to air and
direct sunlight.*

FACING PAGE
*This tagine will be far more
flavoursome if the fish has
been marinated in chermoula,
for several hours.*

Fish couscous

SERVES 8
PREPARATION TIME: 1 HOUR
COOKING TIME: 1–2 HOURS
(DEPENDING ON COUSCOUS CHOICE)

COUSCOUS: (SEE PAGE 150,
OR USE THE PRE-COOKED VARIETY)

BOUILLON INGREDIENTS:
3 LITRES (12½ CUPS) WATER
2 BAY LEAVES
OLIVE OIL
1 BUNCH OF PARSLEY, FINELY CHOPPED
1 BUNCH OF CORIANDER (CILANTRO),
FINELY CHOPPED
150 G (⅔ CUP) CHICKPEAS (GARBANZO BEANS),
SOAKED OVERNIGHT
2 LARGE ONIONS PLUS 1 ONION, THINLY SLICED
2 HOT CHILLIES, WHOLE
10 SMALL TURNIPS, SLICED
8 CARROTS, SLICED
3 COURGETTES (ZUCCHINI), SLICED
4 GARLIC CLOVES, CHOPPED
1 KG (2 LB) RIPE TOMATOES, SKINNED,
DESEEDED AND DICED
2 KG (4 LB) SEA BASS, SEA BREAM (PORGY),
GROUPER, OR PAGEOT (RED SEA BREAM])

Pour the water into the stewing-pan section of the couscousier or a steamer. Add the bay leaves, olive oil (to taste), parsley, coriander (cilantro), chickpeas (garbanzo beans), 2 whole onions, the chillies, turnips, carrots and courgettes (zucchini). Cover, bring to the boil and cook for about 1 hour.

Brown the garlic and the thinly sliced onion in a separate pan in a little oil, add the tomatoes and cook until pulpy.

Poach the fish in the vegetable bouillon until tender. Strain and place the fish on a serving dish and top it with the tomato and onion sauce.

Serve the couscous in a bowl, accompanied by the fish in a separate dish. The bouillon and vegetables can be served in a soup tureen.

Cooking fish in a couscousiere is a delicate process. Depending on its size, the fish is cut into pieces or cooked whole.
The flesh should be firm and the backbone removed. A solution is to cook the fish and couscous separately.

Fish croquettes

SERVES 8
PREPARATION TIME: 30 MINUTES
COOKING TIME: 10 MINUTES EACH

750 G (1½ LB) WHITE FISH
1 ONION, FINELY CHOPPED
2 GARLIC CLOVES, CRUSHED
1 BUNCH OF PARSLEY, FINELY CHOPPED
1 TEASPOON GROUND CUMIN
½ TEASPOON MILD CHILLI POWDER
PINCH OF HOT CHILLI POWDER
SALT
1 BEATEN EGG
1 TABLESPOON OLIVE OIL
2 TABLESPOONS PLAIN (ALL-PURPOSE) FLOUR
OIL FOR FRYING

Clean the fish and pat dry with kitchen paper (paper towels), then remove all the bones.

Finely chop the fish and mix with the onion, garlic, parsley and all the spices. Season with salt.

Bind the mixture with the egg, olive oil and a little water, if necessary, to form a ball. Divide into individual walnut-size croquettes and coat with flour.

Heat the oil in a frying pan (skillet) and fry for 5 minutes on each side.

ABOVE LEFT
*Trawlers moored
in the port of
Mohammedia.*

RIGHT
*Constructed in part
on foundations on
the sea bed,
Casablanca's Hassan
II Mosque is
crowned with
a 200-metre
(650-feet) high
minaret that
overlooks the town.
The esplanade
accommodates a
gathering of around
80,000 faithful.*

FACING PAGE
*The arrival and sale
of fresh fish at
Essaouira, where the
catch may be eaten on
the spot, piping hot
from a grill (broiler).*

Souiri tagine

SERVES 8

PREPARATION TIME: 30 MINUTES

COOKING TIME: 1¼ HOURS

2 x 1.5 KG (3 LB) WHOLE CHICKENS

2 TABLESPOONS MELTED BUTTER

6 TABLESPOONS OIL

1 LARGE ONION, THINLY SLICED

4 GARLIC CLOVES, THINLY SLICED

1 TEASPOON GROUND GINGER

1 PINCH OF SAFFRON

1 TEASPOON PEPPER

8 EGGS

1 TEASPOON SALT

1 BUNCH OF PARSLEY, FINELY CHOPPED

4 TABLESPOONS LEMON JUICE

RIGHT

This chicken tagine is distinctive because the final part of the cooking process is done in the oven, where the sauce turns into a spicy omelette.

Cut the chickens into pieces. Heat the butter and oil in a large, flameproof casserole or stewing pan and add the chicken, onion, garlic and spices. Cover with water and simmer with the lid on over medium heat for about I hour or until the meat is cooked through.

Remove the meat and keep warm in a tagine. Reduce the sauce, then remove from the heat and set aside.

Preheat the oven to 160°C (325°F), Gas Mark 3.

Crack the eggs into a bowl and whisk with a little salt. Add the parsley and lemon juice and mix well.

Pour most of the egg mixture over the chicken and keep the rest in a pan. Put the tagine back in the oven for about 10–15 minutes, checking occasionally. The eggs are better if they are not overcooked. As soon as the egg mix begins to set, remove the tagine from the oven. The eggs will continue to cook gently in the heat absorbed by the tagine. Immediately before serving, heat the rest of the egg mixture and use as a topping. Reheat the sauce and serve separately.

Casserole of pigeon (squab) with dates

Serves 6

Preparation time: 30 minutes

Cooking time: 45 minutes

75 g (6 tablespoons) butter, melted

6 pigeons (squab), giblets removed

3 large onions, thinly sliced

1 garlic clove, crushed

1 teaspoon ground ginger

salt

pinch of saffron

750 g (4 cups) dates, pitted

1 teaspoon ground cinnamon

4 tablespoons honey (preferably acacia)

Melt the butter in a large, wide-based casserole or stewing pan. Place the pigeons (squab) side by side in the pan and add the onions, garlic, ginger, salt and saffron. Cover the contents with cold water and simmer gently, partially covered, for about 30 minutes or until the pigeons (squab) are tender. Add the dates, cinnamon and honey and simmer for a further 15 minutes. Arrange the pigeons in a circle on a serving dish, covered in the onion sauce, with the dates in the middle.

Chicken tagine with dried apricots and raisins

Serves 6

Preparation time: 30 minutes

Cooking time: 1 hour

1 free-range chicken, cut into pieces

4 tablespoons oil

1 large onion, finely chopped

½ teaspoon ground cinnamon + 2 sticks

½ teaspoon ground ginger

½ teaspoon ground pepper

pinch of saffron

1 teaspoon salt

400 ml (1¾ cups) cold water

½ bunch parsley, tied in a bunch

2 tablespoons honey

12 dried apricots

100 g (¾ cup) raisins, rinsed

Clean the chicken pieces and pat dry. Heat the oil in a heavy pan and add the onion, spices and salt. Pour in the water; stir well, add the chicken pieces and bring to the boil. Lower the heat, turn the chicken over in the cooking liquid and add the parsley bunch. Simmer over medium heat, stirring frequently. When the meat begins to fall off the bone, remove the chicken and set aside to keep warm.

Add the honey, apricots and raisins to the pan. Simmer gently, with the lid off, over a very low heat for about 15 minutes, until the sauce is reduced thoroughly and is of a thick consistency.

Arrange the pieces of chicken on a serving dish, accompanied by the dried apricot and raisin sauce.

As with dried figs and prunes, mechmech, small aromatic dried apricots, can enhance any chicken or lamb tagine with their deliciously mild flavour.

Medfoun couscous

SERVES 8–10
PREPARATION TIME: 30 MINUTES
STANDING TIME: 30 MINUTES
COOKING TIME: 1½ HOURS

Nicknamed 'couscous surprise', medfoun couscous is garnished with icing (confectioners') sugar and ground cinnamon. It is usually enjoyed with a glass of fresh milk.

250 G (1 CUP) BUTTER
750 G (1½ LB) BONED LAMB SHOULDER, DICED
5 ONIONS, CHOPPED
SALT
½ TEASPOON PEPPER
GENEROUS PINCH OF SAFFRON
1 TEASPOON GROUND CINNAMON
1 TABLESPOON GROUNDNUT (PEANUT) OIL
1 KG (5⅓ CUPS) MEDIUM GRAIN COUSCOUS
TO GARNISH: CINNAMON AND ICING
(CONFECTIONERS') SUGAR

Heat half the butter in a heavy pan and brown the lamb. Add the onions, salt, pepper, saffron and cinnamon. Cover with water and simmer over medium heat until the water has completely evaporated. Set the pan aside while the couscous is being prepared – see also page 150 or use pre-cooked couscous if time is limited.

Pour the couscous grains into an earthenware bowl, or you could use a wooden *gsââ*, a large, flat wooden dish with a sloping lip. Oil your hands with the groundnut (peanut) oil and work the grains, rubbing them between your fingers and the palms of your hands; the oil should be evenly distributed throughout the grains. Sprinkle a glass of cold water over the grains and lightly rub the mixture between your fingers, using your hands to separate the grains; it should be free from lumps. Leave to stand for 15 minutes.

Repeat the process once more. Cook the couscous in a steamer or the top section of a couscousier for 15 minutes. Spread the couscous in the *gsââ* once again and leave to chill. Work the grains again, this time using a fork. Put the couscous on to cook again in the steamer for 5–10 minutes. Dot the couscous with the remaining butter. The presentation of this dish is different from the usual couscous ring style: Spread a layer of couscous over the base of the serving dish and cover with the meat and sauce. Cover with the remaining couscous, making sure that all the meat and sauce is hidden.

Serve garnished with cinnamon and icing (confectioners') sugar.

فن إعداد المائدة THE ART OF TABLE LAYING

A traditional Moroccan meal is usually a convivial affair, where participants gather together around a low, round dining table, located in a corner of the living room, and sit on long divan-style seats covered with large cushions or pouffes. Embroidered tablecloths have large matching napkins, which diners drape over their knees.

A washstand, *tass*, and ewer, diffusing delicate perfumes of orange-flower or rosewater, waft around the table. Once the master of the house has uttered the sacred word, *Bismillah* (in the Name of Allah), then the meal may commence. Salads are arranged on the table, on small plates, with salt, pepper and cumin placed in hors d'oeuvres dishes. The traditional round loaf, cut into quarters, is passed around in generous quantities. In the absence of spoons, it is the accepted custom for everyone to help themselves from large round serving dishes, placed in the centre of the table, using a piece of bread held between the thumb, forefinger and middle finger of the right hand, to mop up the sauce. The left hand is considered unclean and never used to lift food to the mouth. A pastilla or brochettes, a tagine, or couscous on Fridays, typifies an ordinary meal, which concludes with the arrival of a basket of fruit and the master of the house declaring *Al-Hamdullilah* (Praise be to Allah). It is customary to rinse one's hands again at the end of the meal, and to withdraw to a separate table to enjoy mint tea and sweet pastries.

Refreshing and varied salads arranged on flat plates are offered as appetizers for summertime meals.

Kesraa flavoured with aniseed or sesame is used instead of place settings.

For all masters of the house, hospitality is sacrosanct.

Rose petals scattered over the white embroidered tablecloth adds a touch of elegance to festive meals.

Watermelon and orange salad with cinnamon

No fewer than five varieties of oranges grow in the open countryside around Sous, in the south-west part of Morocco.

SERVES 4

PREPARATION TIME: 20 MINUTES

CHILLING TIME: 2 HOURS

6 ORANGES

1 WATERMELON

3 TABLESPOONS ORANGE-FLOWER WATER

1 TEASPOON GROUND CINNAMON

2 TABLESPOONS SUGAR

FEW MINT LEAVES TO DECORATE

With a sharp knife cut off the peel together with all the white pith from 4 oranges and slice into rounds. Squeeze the juice from the remaining oranges and set aside. Cut the watermelon in half; remove the flesh and cut into cubes. Cover the base of a deep dish with the orange rounds and arrange the watermelon in the centre.

In a separate bowl, mix together the orange-flower water, cinnamon, orange juice and sugar. Pour this mixture over the fruit and decorate with mint leaves.

Chill in the refrigerator for at least 2 hours before serving.

ORANGE-FLOWER WATER

ماء الزهر

The perfume from the fine droplets of orange-flower water that are wafted around using a scent spray with a long nozzle acts as a prelude to the pleasures of mealtime. Orange-flower water has a calming effect, its scent fills the air; it also adds flavour to recipes, milk, sweet pastries and confectionery. A bride's hair is sprayed with orange-flower water and it is sprinkled on the tombs of the deceased; people splash it on their hands and faces as a symbol of purity on important festive occasions. Gathered in springtime, the flowers of bitter-tasting bigarade oranges are distilled in an alembic still, called a *quettara*. A kilo (2 lb) of flowers produces around two litres (8¾ cups) of orange-flower water. In the bottom section of the alembic, the water is brought to boiling point, while the flowers are placed in a basket in the centre of the still. The top section, which is fitted with two large tubes, is filled with cold water. The first tube collects the steam from the water that passes through the petals and cools it. This enables the perfumed water to fall, drop by drop, into the bottle placed at the end of the tube. The other tube is designed to empty the water as soon as it reheats and to replace the hot water with cold. As soon as the bottles are full, they are hermetically sealed and stored out of direct light.

Gors
(brioche)

MAKES 12
PREPARATION TIME: 1 HOUR
STANDING TIME: 4 HOURS
COOKING TIME: 30 MINUTES

1 KG (8 CUPS) PLAIN (ALL-PURPOSE) FLOUR
PINCH OF SALT
200 G (1 CUP) CASTER (SUPERFINE) SUGAR
2 BEATEN EGGS + 1 EGG YOLK
2 TEASPOONS FENNEL SEEDS
200 G (SCANT 1 CUP) BUTTER, MELTED
½ TEASPOON GROUND GUM ARABIC
1 LITRE (4 CUPS) MILK
100 G (3½ OZ) BAKER'S YEAST
2 TEASPOONS SESAME SEEDS

Place the flour in a large mixing bowl with the salt, sugar, 2 eggs, fennel seeds, butter and gum arabic.

Boil the milk and set aside to cool.

Dilute the yeast in a separate small bowl, using some of the lukewarm milk and add to the mixing bowl. (If using fresh yeast, leave to rise for 10–15 minutes before adding to the bowl). Mix all the ingredients together carefully, gradually folding in the rest of the lukewarm milk. Knead the dough until it becomes smooth and elastic, but doesn't stick to your hands. Form into a large ball.

Dust the ball of dough with flour and place in a clean mixing bowl, cover with a tea towel (dishcloth) or clingfilm (plastic wrap) and leave to rise in a warm place for about 2 hours.

Knead the dough again. Divide into small, tangerine-size balls, and flatten with the palm of the hand. Place the dough rounds on a baking (cookie) sheet and cover as before. Leave to rise for a further 2 hours, in a warm place.

Preheat the oven to 220°C (425°F), Gas Mark 7.

Beat the egg yolk with a little water and glaze the dough balls. Sprinkle with sesame seeds and bake for about 30 minutes. The brioches should appear golden brown and well risen.

Rghaïfs with eggs

SERVES 6
PREPARATION TIME: 20 MINUTES
COOKING TIME: 5 MINUTES EACH

3 EGGS
6 SHEETS FILO PASTRY (OR 12 SHEETS BRIK)
OIL FOR FRYING
2 TABLESPOONS ICING (CONFECTIONERS') SUGAR
1 TEASPOON GROUND CINNAMON

Pancakes, brioches and small almond cakes are common to all regions of Morocco. They are particularly evident on festive occasions, accompanied by mint tea or served for breakfast.

Break the eggs into a bowl and whisk them briskly.

Cut 12 x 20-cm (8-inch) squares from the 6 sheets of filo pastry.

Brush each pastry sheet with beaten egg; fold into half and then into half again to form squares.

Heat the oil in a frying pan (skillet) and when it is sizzling hot fry the squares, one at a time. Fry until the underneath is golden brown and crisp, while basting the top with the hot oil. Flip over and cook for about 2 minutes more. Repeat for the remaining squares.

Depending on the size of your frying pan (skillet), you may be able to fry several rghaïfs at the same time.

Blot the rghaïfs with kitchen paper (paper towels) and serve hot, dusted with icing (confectioners') sugar and ground cinnamon.

EARTHENWARE الخزف المطلي

In pride of place, in the centre of low round tables throughout the land, the *tagine slaoui* (also referred to simply as 'tagine'), a round terracotta dish produced in the town of Salé, always presides at mealtimes. The tagine is heat-resistant and its conical-shaped glazed lid helps keep the food hot. It is used to cook tagine dishes, egg kefta croquettes or *khlii* (sun-dried, preserved meat) dishes with eggs. The most commonly used serving dishes are *taous* — large round dishes made of porcelain, or colour-coordinated earthenware dishes that match the table setting. Small plates are used to serve salads; bowls are laid out for serving soups. It is possible to identify where specific glazed earthenware items have been produced from their decorative styles and colours. Fès ceramics are predominantly cobalt blue in colour and are the most sophisticated, drawing their inspiration from geometric and floral, stylized or sophisticated, motifs. Salé pottery is identified by its pastel shades of pink, pale green and blue, whereas the polychrome motifs of Safi earthenware are derived from Berber decorative designs, patterns that change over the years, according to the artistic whims of their creators. Ornate urban-influenced pottery contrasts with simple rustic shaped Berber terracotta earthenware, decorated in hues of ochre and brown. Practical and functional, Berber pottery is produced mainly for domestic use: bowls, butter dishes, milk jugs (pitchers), jars, water jugs (pitchers), long-necked pitchers...

FACING PAGE
A butter pot from a Fès pottery.

Berber pottery is either produced by men using a potter's wheel or moulded by hand by the women. Amphorae, earthenware jugs (pitchers), dishes and plates are needed for practical purposes; decoration is secondary.

In Safi, patterned glazed earthenware, based on a curved design, offers perfect symmetry and comes in a variety of bright colours.

These round-based terracotta jars with ochre and brown decoration, produced in the Atlas region, are not free-standing and need to be supported on tripods.

Marrakech
and the South

Marrakech, an exuberant city, open to all, renowned for its gentle way of life and the human warmth of its inhabitants, is a melting pot for Arab, Berber and sub-Saharan cultures. According to the legend, the palm groves of Marrakech sprang up as a result of date pits thrown away by the soldiers of Youssef ben Tachfine, founder of the city around the year 1062. The city's artificial lake

ABOVE

This vast reservoir supplies water to the gardens of Menara, which is planted with hundreds of olive trees. In its depth, you can see the reflection of a romantic Saadian pavilion.

RIGHT

In Marrakech, the shoemakers' stalls are stocked with gaily patterned slippers and sandals.

certainly owes its existence to the gigantic irrigation works that were ordered by the sultan, and the underground canal system, supplied by wells, that water the grandiose gardens of the city. The Almoravids, then the Almohads, made Marrakech their capital, but the city was shunned by the Merinids, who preferred to live in the city of Fès. During the sixteenth century, the 'Red City' of Marrakech regained its role as capital city. Situated alongside the trail that formerly linked the Atlantic with black Africa, the city grew rich from the gold brought back from the Sudan by expeditions across the Sahara. Imposing public buildings bear testimony to those former days. The palaces are adorned in marble, stucco, ivory and ebony.

Tourists should visit the ancient site for public executions, Jemaa el Fnaa square (the 'Assembly' or 'Parade' of the Dead), that conjures up the pace of life and

activities of the ancient imperial city as it existed in years gone by. Dominated by the Koutoubia Mosque, at the heart of the city, the square is a continual real live stage upon which the drama of Marrakech life is played out today.

From early morning onwards, the square is packed with brightly coloured awnings, pyramids of fruit and vegetables, herbs and poultry. In the afternoon, the entertainers, scribes, acrobats, snake charmers, jugglers and monkey trainers besiege the square and entertain the crowds. Water carriers, characters that typify the Jemaa el Fnaa square, stroll around, drawing water from their animal skin containers to quench the thirst of passers-by. Copper goblets hang around their necks, clanking up and down on their red costumes, swaying to the rhythm of the multi-coloured fringes of their large hats. At dusk, when the crimson sky casts its final glowing rays over Jemaa el Fnaa, the square is transformed into a massive open-air restaurant. A colourfully dressed crowd pushes its way into the centre from every direction and gathers around the braziers and gas-fired lanterns. Strolling 'restaurateurs', dressed entirely in white, pitch their 'kitchens' amid an impromptu, rectangular space marked out by a few tables and benches. Stalls, grouped according to the types of produce they sell, offer rows of spiced liver, grilled (broiled) sole, bowls of harira, fried aubergines (eggplant), tagines, chickens in curcurma — turmeric.

Subject to seasonal variations and the huge differences in temperature, Berber-influenced Marrakech cuisine is varied and offers a huge diversity of dishes. Thick, warm, nourishing soups for cold winter nights contrast with numerous colourful salads, flavoured with refreshing garlic and cumin, that cool the overheated palate during the hot summer. One of the specialities of Marrakech and its surrounding area is *tangia marrakchia*, an aromatic lamb or veal-based dish: another is *makfoul*, a lamb, tomato and onion tagine, spiced with saffron, cinnamon, chilli, ginger and honey.

Otherwise, the inhabitants of the Atlas Mountains lead a frugal existence, where daily life revolves around the changing seasons. Ploughing, chopping wood, harvesting olives, almonds, walnuts, reaping maize (corn), sorting turnips… punctuate the agricultural calendar. Villages sometimes lead a virtually autonomous existence. The same forces drive the Berber communities, who store up reserves for the following winter to make sure that their families survive. For the rest of the people, who dwell in the upper valleys of the Atlas Mountains, their sole means of subsistence consists of small plots growing wheat, barley, maize (corn), broad (fava) beans, marrows (zucchini), turnips, onions and potatoes. Their diet varies little from day to day: turnip, carrot, potato tagines; on festive occasions with added pieces of lamb, barley semolina, sprinkled with melted rancid butter thrown in for good measure; couscous without meat and, of course, bread, the basis of every meal, soaked in honey or olive oil, accompanied by tea or coffee. In the basic kitchens of the High Atlas Mountains, where whole families gather during extremely cold weather, openings in the walls are uncommon, and where they do exist, are very small, with the chimney typically positioned in the centre of the room. In general, several braziers are always burning and constantly stoked, one to heat the water boiler for the tea, the other to provide heat for the tagine *slaoui* (rounded earthenware pot with

In the imperial cities, in numerous sanctuaries, shoes are removed before entering a mosque or before treading on a carpet in a house.

In the south of Morocco, tall dunes rise up out of the stony desert. From January onwards storks perch on the tops of minarets. Young Berber girls copy their mothers' mannerisms from a very early age.

glazed pointed lid). The women move from one brazier to the next. To make bread, wheat and bran flour is sifted through a flour riddle made of wood and tightly woven wire mesh. The women then knead the flour and water, backwards and forwards with the palms of their hands, in a large wooden bowl, to produce thick elastic dough. The huge ball of dough is then used to make

are cultivated, as well as a few patches of pungent-flowered, henna bushes. Once harvested and ground to a powder, the colourful small leaves of the henna plant are used to paint sophisticated designs on the hands and feet of the women.

The Berbers are the couscous specialists, consuming mainly barley-based semolina, accompanied by steamed turnip leaves or chopped alfalfa.

several loaves of bread. Plaited (braided) lumps of risen dough disappear into the hot glowing embers of the braziers or into an igloo-shaped oven constructed of dried mud and built into the ground, fuelled by roots and dried herbs.

By shaking the contents of goatskin containers hanging from hooks, fresh milk is turned into curdled butter, which retains the strong flavour of the goatskins in which it has been stored.

Life is equally precarious in the oases of the south, despite the less harsh climate, compared with the mountainous regions. In the stony desert, punctuated by green oases and steep canyons that emerge at the edge of the Atlas Mountains, the *oueds* or *wadis* (seasonal rivers) mark out a pathway all the way to the Sahara.

The natural resources of these oases, the date palm trees that shelter peach trees in their shadow, pomegranate or fig trees and small plots of barley, wheat, alfalfa,

Méchoui (barbecue of a whole roast sheep) is another speciality, reserved for festive occasions. Cooked outdoors, by the men only, the lamb is coated with a melted butter, pepper, coriander and salt sauce and roasted on a spit, over braziers.

Staple foods in the Saharan regions consist of dates, which are highly nutritious, easy to transport and preserve, camel's milk, *smen*, rancid clarified butter that keeps for several months in preserving jars, camel's meat, goat's meat and mutton. Fish is a commodity that is virtually unheard of. The Saharan version of couscous is accompanied by small, semi-preserved, wild figs. Saharan hospitality is legendary, with guests being offered countless glasses of tea. In these regions, custom dictates that one accepts three glasses of tea, in straight succession.

LEFT
The adobe villages of the Dadès Valley, are arranged along the oued *or* wadi *(seasonal river), bordering on to minute patches of cultivated land.*

ABOVE
A dromedary made out of reeds, woven by children from the southern oases.

In the souk trading quarter of Marrakech, merchants offer every spice conceivable, from all around the world, while the apothecaries extol the virtues of their medicinal herbs, cures for all types of rheumatism or snoring... Dried lizards' tails, live chameleons, stuffed birds are offered by way of lucky charms. Further on, displays are crammed with beauty products such as kohl and henna, or walnut bark, used to whiten teeth.

Tomato coulis

MAKES ABOUT 2.5 LITRES (10 CUPS)
PREPARATION TIME: 15 MINUTES
COOKING TIME: 3 HOURS

4 KG (8 LB) RIPE TOMATOES
6 CLOVES GARLIC, CRUSHED
2 TEASPOONS GROUND CINNAMON
1 TEASPOON GROUND GINGER
1 TEASPOON HOT OR MILD CHILLI POWDER
SALT
2 TABLESPOONS CASTER (SUPERFINE) SUGAR

Chop the tomatoes into large chunks and reduce to a purée in a food processor or blender. Transfer the purée into a large, heavy pan and stir in the garlic, cinnamon, ginger, chilli powder and salt. Cook over medium to high heat for about 1 hour, stirring frequently to prevent the coulis from sticking.

Lower the heat and simmer gently over low heat for up to 2 hours, or until all the water has evaporated. Continue cooking until the mixture has reached the required consistency.

Finally, stir in the sugar and mix well.

Caramelized tomatoes

These cooked tomatoes, sweetened with sugar and honey, are equally delicious served hot or cold, in a salad or as an accompaniment for meat.

Serves 4

Preparation time: 20 minutes

Cooking time: 30 minutes

8 very ripe tomatoes

2 tablespoons oil

Salt

2 tablespoons caster (superfine) sugar

¼ teaspoon ground cinnamon

¼ tablespoon ground pepper

1 tablespoon honey

Place the tomatoes in a bowl and pour in boiling water to cover. Leave for 1–2 minutes, then drain, cut a cross at the stem end and peel off the skins. Cut the tomatoes in half. Heat the oil in a flameproof casserole or heavy pan; add the tomatoes, salt and sugar. Cook for about 30 minutes or until all the liquid has been absorbed. Add the cinnamon, pepper and honey and mix together.

Broad (fava) bean bessara

SERVES 4

PREPARATION TIME: 5 MINUTES

COOKING TIME: 1¼ HOURS

250 G (8 OZ) DRIED BROAD (FAVA) BEANS,
SOAKED OVERNIGHT

2 LITRES (8¾ CUPS) WATER

2 TABLESPOONS OLIVE OIL

4 CLOVES GARLIC, WHOLE

½ TEASPOON GROUND CUMIN

½ TEASPOON MILD CHILLI POWDER

OLIVE OIL

SALT

ABOVE

*Fresh broad (fava)
beans are seasonal
vegetables and are
available at market
from May onwards.
If the skins are too
tough, they can easily
be removed after
blanching in boiling
water.*

Drain the broad (fava) beans and remove
the outer skins.

Bring 2 litres (8¾ cups) of salted water
to the boil in a large pan. Add the oil,
garlic cloves and broad (fava) beans.
Cover the pan and simmer over medium
heat for 1 hour. Stir the contents and
continue simmering, over low heat, until
the consistency is smooth.

Just before serving, transfer the mixture
to a deep serving dish, sprinkle with the
ground cumin and chilli powder and
drizzle with a little olive oil. Season with
salt to taste.

This recipe can also be made using
split peas or chickpeas (garbanzo beans)
instead of broad (fava) beans.

Sweet potatoes with raisins

Serves 6
Preparation time: 15 minutes
Cooking time: 20 minutes

1 kg (2 lb) sweet potatoes, peeled
250 g (1⅔ cups) seedless raisins
100 ml (scant ½ cup) oil
½ teaspoon ground pepper
1 clove garlic, crushed
1–2 teaspoons ground cinnamon
salt

Cut the sweet potatoes into large chunks. Place them in a pan with the rest of the ingredients and pour in 500 ml (generous 2 cups) water. Cook over medium heat for 15–20 minutes or until the potatoes are tender and the liquid reduced. Serve hot or cold.

Sweet potato m'chermla

Serves 6
Preparation time: 15 minutes
Cooking time: 20 minutes

1 kg (2 lb) sweet potatoes, peeled
4 cloves garlic, crushed
2 tablespoons chopped coriander (cilantro)
100 ml (scant ½ cup) olive oil
½ teaspoon mild chilli powder
1 teaspoon ground cumin
1 teaspoon caster (superfine) sugar
pinch of saffron
salt

Cut the sweet potatoes into large chunks. Place them in a pan with the rest of the ingredients and pour in 500 ml (generous 2 cups) water. Cook over medium heat for 15–20 minutes or until the potatoes are tender and the liquid reduced. Serve hot or cold.

Brania with cinnamon
(fried aubergines [eggplant] with cinnamon)

SERVES 6

PREPARATION TIME: 20 MINUTES

STANDING TIME: 30 MINUTES

COOKING TIME: 35 MINUTES

1 KG (2 LB) AUBERGINES (EGGPLANT)

COARSE SALT

3 EGG WHITES

OIL FOR FRYING

1 TEASPOON GROUND CINNAMON

2 TABLESPOONS SUGAR

Cut the aubergines (eggplant) into rounds, about 1-cm (½-inch) thick. Place the rounds in a strainer and sprinkle over with the salt. Leave for 30 minutes to draw out the bitter liquid. Rinse, drain and blot with kitchen paper (paper towels). Whisk the egg whites lightly with a fork and dip each round to coat thoroughly.

Heat the oil in a frying pan (skillet) and when the oil is sizzling hot, fry the aubergine (eggplant) rounds on both sides for a few minutes. Drain on kitchen paper (paper towels).

Arrange the aubergines (eggplant) in a tagine or a large cooking pan and dust with the cinnamon and sugar. Sprinkle 4 tablespoons of water on top and cook over low heat for 30 minutes or until the sauce is thick.

Okra purée

SERVES 6

PREPARATION TIME: 20 MINUTES

COOKING TIME: 30 MINUTES

1 KG (2 LB) OKRA

2 TEASPOONS OLIVE OIL

1 TEASPOON SALT

1 TEASPOON GROUND PEPPER

1 ONION, THINLY SLICED

1 BUNCH OF PARSLEY, CHOPPED

1 BUNCH OF CORIANDER (CILANTRO), CHOPPED

Remove the okra stalks. Place the oil, salt, pepper, okra and onion in a large pan and cook, stirring constantly, over high heat. Add the parsley and coriander (cilantro) and continue to cook until the okra is tender.

Remove from the heat and mash with a fork or with a pestle and mortar or process in a food processor or blender. Adjust the seasoning to taste.

Serve hot or cold, with a slice of lemon for extra flavour.

FACING PAGE, ABOVE
Preparing okra. Much sought after by the Marrakshis, as well as the Fassi, this vegetable, produced by a plant with yellow flowers, of Indian origin, cooks quickly.

FACING PAGE, BELOW
Flat leaf parsley and coriander (cilantro) are used together, in quite large quantities, in numerous recipes.

Tomato salad with mint

SERVES 6

PREPARATION TIME: 15 MINUTES

Extra virgin olive oil, produced in the major cities of Morocco, enhances raw and cooked vegetables with its flavour.

6 LARGE, RIPE TOMATOES

1 ONION (PREFERABLY WHITE), SHREDDED

1 TABLESPOON CHOPPED PARSLEY

1 TABLESPOON COARSELY CHOPPED MINT

4 TABLESPOONS LEMON JUICE

2 TABLESPOONS OLIVE OIL

SALT

¼ TABLESPOON GROUND PEPPER

PINCH OF ICING (CONFECTIONERS') SUGAR

Place the tomatoes in a bowl and pour in boiling water to cover. Leave to stand for 1–2 minutes, then drain, cut a cross at the stem end and peel off the skins. Cut in half and deseed, cut into pieces. Drain using a fine strainer.

Place the onion and drained tomatoes in a salad bowl; add the parsley and mint. Sprinkle with the lemon juice, oil, salt and pepper. A pinch of icing (confectioners') sugar will reduce the pungency of the onion.

OLIVE OIL زيت الزيتون

There are several thousand *maasras* located across the countryside of Morocco. These oil mills still use age-old processing techniques to extract precious oil from the olive harvest. In the autumn (fall), green, black and purple olives are harvested in large wicker baskets. The flavour and fruitiness of the final product is dependent upon the blend of olives used to process the oil. Five kilos (10 lb) of olives are required to produce one litre (4 cups) of oil. Inside the oil mills, donkeys are used to turn the grindstones that crush the olives, flesh and pits, under their heavy weight. The resulting dark-coloured pulp is placed in large, porous, flat baskets made of plaited (braided) esparto grass, the *scourtins*, which are then stacked one on top of another, ready to slide under the press. The pressing process releases the oil, which then flows into tanks where it is allowed to settle. Once the water sinks to the bottom of the tanks, the oil can be drawn off the surface. The luminous oil, with a distinctive taste, is destined for domestic consumption and is stored in watertight, earthenware jars and used in couscous, frying and omelettes, or simply for dunking bread at breakfast. Certain large-scale industrial plants, at Fès, Marrakech, and Meknès produce and bottle extra virgin olive oil, on site, for the export market.

SPICES التوابل

The Egyptians used cinnamon, over three thousand years ago, to perfume incense and ointments. The history of spices abounds with legendary tales of distant explorations. Aromas of spices permeate the souks; in kitchens you are invited on a voyage of discovery that conjures up the perfumes of the East. Laid out in small, conical-shaped piles in wicker baskets, spices are sold loose. The red colour of paprika, the golden hues of saffron, the ochre shades of cinnamon, nutmeg and cumin, the bright beige of ginger, all create a colourful mosaic. Each spice is imbued with its distinctive digestive qualities and health-giving and stimulating properties. Saffron, cumin, coriander, chilli powder and fenugreek are cultivated on Moroccan soil. Cinnamon, ginger and cloves are imported from the East. Cinnamon is used in stick or powder form, its mild sweetness adding flavour to pastilla, oranges, semolina and certain sweetened tagines. Cumin is used to coat grilled (broiled) meat brochettes and to flavour eggs and salads. Ginger, with its intense aroma, goes well in both sweet and savoury dishes; red chilli powder is eaten either mild or hot, depending on the household's preferences. Toasted sesame seeds are sprinkled on tagines and cakes; dried aniseed seeds add aroma to bread rolls; caraway seeds add superb flavour to soups.

Only the bark of the cinnamon trees of Sri Lanka is capable of producing authentic cinnamon, which comes in the shape of small sticks that roll up during the drying process.

Cinnamon is harvested during the wet season, when the bark is easy to peel off the trees.

CURRY POWDER

NIGELLA

Curry powder is a blend of spices and is made up according to a grocer's specific recipe, which typically comprises coriander, cumin, ginger, pepper, turmeric and, occasionally, cinnamon, cloves and nutmeg.

Product of the nigella flower, dubbed 'Love-in-the-Mist', nigella seeds are shaped like brown tears. They are often mixed with onion or mustard seeds. Roasted before grinding, they exude a peppery and lemony aroma.

TURMERIC

CARAWAY

SAFFRON THREADS

Similar to ginger, turmeric is a rhizome, originally from southern India. Piquant, with a mild peppery flavour, it is sold in powder form and lends a delightful yellow colour to curries and any dish where it is used to enhance the flavour.

Originally from northern Europe and Asia, caraway seeds are used whole in Morocco as an ingredient in cakes, breads and certain soups.

The stigma of the crocus flower, which are dried and sold as threads, are used to add colour and aroma to recipes. Because saffron is the most expensive of spices, it tends to be used very sparingly.

Kamoun, Moroccan cumin, is generally sold in powder form.

Similar in shape and size to peppercorns, coriander seeds give off a flavour of orange peel. But the seeds of the coriander plant are less aromatic than its fresh leaves, which are used more widely in Moroccan cooking.

Derived from the grains of a member of the umbelliferae family, cumin possesses a slightly bitter-sweet flavour that will perk up any bland-tasting dishes.

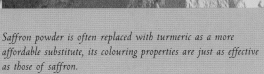

Saffron powder is often replaced with turmeric as a more affordable substitute, its colouring properties are just as effective as those of saffron.

This grocer's secret blend is based on cumin, pepper and mild chilli powder.

Courgettes (zucchini) with cumin

Serves 6
Preparation time: 10 minutes
Cooking time: 15 minutes

750 g (1½ lb) courgettes (zucchini)
1 tablespoon olive oil
2 cloves garlic, crushed
salt
1 teaspoon ground cumin
1 teaspoon ground chilli powder
½ bunch of parsley, chopped
1 bunch of coriander (cilantro), chopped
2 tablespoons lemon juice

Pour 1 litre (4 cups) water into a large pan with a little salt. Add the courgettes (zucchini), whole, and bring to the boil. Reduce the heat and cook for 5 minutes. Drain the courgettes (zucchini) and cut into rounds. In a separate, heavy pan, heat the oil, over low heat, with the garlic. Add 100 ml (scant ½ cup) hot water, 1 teaspoon salt, the cumin, chilli powder, parsley and coriander (cilantro). Bring to the boil.
Add the courgettes (zucchini) and simmer gently for about 5 minutes or until tender. Sprinkle with lemon juice. Serve cold.

Once washed and grated, carrots should be split down the middle, to remove the centre, if it is too tough. In tagines or couscous dishes, carrots are usually cut into four, lengthwise, then each piece is cut in two.

Salad of cooked carrot with chermoula

Serves 4
Preparation time: 20 minutes
Cooking time: 30 minutes

500 g (1 lb) carrots
3 tablespoons chermoula (see page 102)
salt

Pour 1 litre (4 cups) water into a large pan and season with salt. Add the whole carrots and bring to the boil. Reduce the heat and cook for 15–20 minutes.
Drain the carrots and cut into rounds. In a separate pan, dilute the chermoula with 4 tablespoons cold water. Bring to the boil and add the carrots. With the lid off, reduce the mixture over low heat until the liquid has all been absorbed. Serve hot or cold.

Note: This recipe can be made using other vegetables, in particular:
Potatoes: cut into chunks and cook the raw potato in the chermoula;
Courgettes (zucchini): cut into cubes and cook raw in the chermoula;
Broad (fava) beans: cook raw in the chermoula;
Cauliflower and broccoli florets: blanch before cooking in the chermoula.

SEMO أسمدة INAS

In couscous, cereal grains rule supreme, and how it is handled determines the success of the final dish. Hard – durum – wheat is the essential cereal in couscous. In the mountain regions, however, and in the oases, couscous is also made with barley or cornmeal, cultivated on small plots of land. At threshing time in the villages, wooden pitchforks separate the grain, bran and straw. Once it has been sifted and bagged up, the grain is then transported to the watermill, which has largely replaced the basic domestic millstone of two stones, one on top of the other and a drainage channel. The mills in the cities are fully automated. Producing couscous grains by hand, as in the past, is a highly skilled operation that demands long hours of patient preparation. The grains are prepared and rolled from hard-wheat semolina and hard-wheat flour. In a large, round wooden container or in a glazed earthenware *gsââ*, the cook slowly and carefully sprinkles the semolina flour with salted water, rolls it for a long time, using the palms of the hands and circular movements, until the grains are coated with a fine film and are all separated and lump-free. The grains are then poured into a *tbaq*, a wicker basket with a spiral-shaped base where the grains are riddled and separate off, naturally, according to their size. The finest grains are left to dry for a while before repeating the rolling process, but this time incorporating a few pinches of flour and a sprinkling of water to make the grains finer. They are then sifted through several sieves in turn to remove the flour and the grains that are too fine, until the grains that remain are of a perfect grade. The grains that have passed 'quality control' are then placed in the sun to dry, while the residue is worked again. The size of the grain depends on the cereal used for grinding. Nowadays, mechanical rolling produces three types of couscous: fine, medium and coarse.

Depending on the region, couscous is made from hard wheat, barley, rye or cornmeal, and flour.

Dried vegetables feature prominently in the large souks. Before being cooked in couscous recipes, chickpeas (garbanzo beans) are soaked in water for several hours, then peeled.

Traditional method of preparing couscous

Place the couscous grains in a *gsââ* – glazed earthenware dish – or a large mixing bowl. Sprinkle with water and rub lightly with the fingertips to separate the grains.

Repeat the process and leave the grains to swell up for about 10–15 minutes.

Pour the couscous into the top section of an oiled couscousier or steamer, above the bouillon and cook. Once all the liquid has turned to steam and escaped, from the top part of the couscousier, remove the metal sieve and tip the couscous back into the *gsââ*. Separate the grains using oiled hands or with a large, oiled wooden spoon. Then replace the grains in the top section of the couscousier.

After a further 20 minutes cooking over bouillon, repeat the process.

Make sure that the couscous does not become too dry; add a little water, if required. Replace the couscous in the top part of the couscousier (at this point, you should place the vegetables in the lower section and allow them to cook through). The grains will continue to cook above, in the steam created by the vegetables cooking below.

When everything is cooked through, roll the couscous manually, using fingers and palms, rubbing in some butter to help separate and enrich the grains.

Arrange the couscous in the middle of the serving dish. Make a well in the centre, using a small, round bowl to create a neat circular depression. Place the meat in the centre and cover with the vegetables. Sprinkle with the vegetable bouillon.

Serve immediately, piping hot, with a bowl of bouillon accompanied by a serving spoon for guests to help themselves.

Note: Ready-made couscous is available at most large supermarkets. All you need to do is moisten the couscous and steam or follow the instructions on the packet.

Belboula

Belboula is a type of couscous made from flour and hard wheat or barley semolina.

PREPARATION TIME: 30 MINUTES
COOKING TIME: 1½ HOURS

BARLEY SEMOLINA

Handle the barley semolina like the wheat semolina used for couscous (see above). The bouillon is prepared in the same way as for lamb couscous with vegetables (see page 153) but using beef, pumpkin, green beans and 2–3 hot, fresh chillies, served whole.

Beef with whole-wheat couscous

Serves 8
Preparation time: 45 minutes
Cooking time: 1½ hours

375 g (1½ cups) chickpeas (garbanzo beans),
soaked overnight
250 g (1¼ cups) dried broad (fava) beans,
soaked overnight (see Note)
2 kg (4 lb) stewing beef, diced
2 large onions, chopped
1 teaspoon mild chilli powder
1 bunch of parsley, chopped
salt, ground pepper
1 kg (5⅓ cups) whole-wheat couscous
500 g (1 lb) pumpkin, unpeeled, cut into
large chunks
500 g (1 lb) turnips, peeled and sliced
2–3 hot chillies, whole (optional)
olive oil or butter

Pour 3 litres (12½ cups) water into a large, heavy pan or the bottom section of a couscousier or steamer. Add the chickpeas (garbanzo beans), broad (fava) beans, diced beef, onions, chilli powder, parsley and salt and pepper. Mix well and cook for about 1 hour.

Prepare the whole-wheat couscous from the recipe on page 150, or use ready-made.

After the meat has been cooking for 1 hour, add the pumpkin, turnips, chillies (if using) and continue to cook until tender.

Serve the couscous coated in olive oil or butter, topped with the cooked beef and vegetables and drenched generously with the bouillon.

Note: If using frozen or fresh broad (fava) beans, add them with the pumpkin and turnips.

Couscous with lamb and vegetables

SERVES 10

PREPARATION TIME: 1 HOUR

COOKING TIME: 1½ HOURS

1 BONED SHOULDER OF LAMB, DICED

150 G (⅔ CUP) CHICKPEAS (GARBANZO BEANS), SOAKED OVERNIGHT

3 LARGE ONIONS, THINLY SLICED

2 LEEKS, SLICED

½ BUNCH OF CELERY, CHOPPED

OLIVE OIL

SALT

1 TEASPOON GROUND PEPPER

1 TEASPOON GROUND GINGER

½ TEASPOON SAFFRON

1 KG (5⅓ CUPS) FINE COUSCOUS

100 ML (SCANT ½ CUP) VEGETABLE OIL

1 GREEN (BELL) PEPPER, DESEEDED AND DICED

1 RED (BELL) PEPPER, DESEEDED AND DICED

500 G (1 LB) CARROTS, SLICED

500 G (1 LB) TURNIPS, SLICED

1 AUBERGINE (EGGPLANT), SLICED

500 G (1 LB) COURGETTES (ZUCCHINI), SLICED

½ GREEN CABBAGE, CHOPPED

½ BUNCH OF FLAT LEAF PARSLEY, CHOPPED

½ BUNCH OF CORIANDER (CILANTRO), CHOPPED

100 G (¾ CUP) RAISINS

HARISSA (OPTIONAL)

Soak the diced lamb in salted water for 15 minutes, then drain. Drain the chickpeas (garbanzos) and place in the cooking section of the couscousier or steamer together with the onions, leeks, celery, lamb and olive oil and salt to taste. Add 200 ml (scant 1 cup) water or more if necessary. Mix well and bring to the boil.

When the onions are blanched, add the spices and 1 litre (4 cups) hot water. Cover and cook briskly for 30 minutes.

Meanwhile, pour the couscous grains into a basin, season with salt and drizzle with vegetable oil. Moisten with 200 ml scant 1 cup) cold, salted water using the fingers and palms of the hands with a rolling motion to separate the grains.

Place the grains in the steamer section of the couscousier and cook for 20 minutes, uncovered, timed from the point when the steam permeates the grains.

When cooked, pour the couscous into bowl, sprinkle with a little cold water. Use a fork to fluff up the grains thoroughly and leave to cool.

Adjust the seasoning of the bouillon. Depending on the cooking time add, in stages, the prepared (bell) peppers, carrots, turnips, aubergine (eggplant), then the courgettes (zucchini), cabbage, parsley and coriander (cilantro). Return the couscous to the top section of the couscousier or steamer and continue cooking so that it absorbs the flavours from the meat and vegetable mixture cooking below.

When the couscous is cooked, place on a serving dish, drizzle with olive oil and form into a dome shape. Make a well in the centre, add the lamb and cover with the vegetables and raisins. Sprinkle with the bouillon, but make sure it doesn't overflow. The remaining bouillon and any meat and vegetables can be served in a soup tureen. Finally, serve the harissa, if using, in a separate bowl.

LEFT

Eating couscous without a spoon is not for the novice. It involves grasping small pieces of meat with three fingers of the right hand and putting them effortlessly into your mouth.

BREAD الخبز

Kesra, the round-shaped loaf that is baked daily in every home, is a prerequisite on every table, throughout the land. In rural areas, it serves as a meal in itself, dipped in olive oil, rancid butter, *smen* or runny honey. From early morning women can be seen sifting hard-wheat flour or, in the mountain regions, cornmeal or barley. Cooked in a separate bread oven or in the embers of a brazier, the large flat rounds of dough are sometimes taken to the local bakery for baking in the communal wood-burning oven, where one can enjoy the constant waft of warm baked bread. First thing each morning, in the medinas, a stream of young girls comes and goes, balancing wooden planks on their heads bearing rows of *kesras* covered with linen cloth. Each home offers its personal twist to the recipe, by incorporating aniseed grains, sesame, cumin or caraway or by stamping their thumbprint in the uncooked dough or using a unique wooden seal to make sure that there's no mix-up when their bread comes out of the oven! A token of sharing and conviviality, bread is sacred and treated with great respect; it is also considered the bearer of *baraka* good fortune. In the home, the *tbika*, a traditional round, rigid esparto grass wicker basket with a lid shaped like a pointed hat, protects the *kesras* from the humidity and dust.

Beghirs, with their distinctive fine 'honeycomb' appearance, are consumed hot, topped with honey and butter.

Shaping bread dough or thin sheets of brik pastry, one by one, is the daily lot of Moroccan women.

Each area of the medina, where women gather every morning to collect their supplies, has its own type of bread flour.

Bread is sacred and treated with great respect; it is never thrown around casually. If a piece is found on the ground, it is picked up and placed on high.

Some families still produce their own flour, selecting the grain which is then taken to the mill for grinding.

Harking back to the time of French rule, bread in the form of baguettes is only produced in city bakeries and does not play a part in the daily lives of the Moroccan people.

LEFT
Life in Moroccan villages such as Rissani, on the edge of the Sahara, centres upon the weekly souks that take place in the morning.

RIGHT
Tucked away in the glowing embers, the tangia is an earthenware container (see previous page) which is left to cook for hours on end in the bakery oven.

Tangia

SERVES 6

COOKING TIME: 6 HOURS

1.5 KG (3 LB) LAMB
100 G (SCANT ½ CUP) BUTTER
2 TABLESPOONS GROUND CUMIN
2 ONIONS, FINELY CHOPPED
2 CLOVES GARLIC, CRUSHED
200 ML (SCANT 1 CUP) WATER

Spicy lamb- or veal-based tangia is a typical Marrakech dish that is especially favoured by the students and intellectuals of the *médersa*, because it is so tasty and easy to make and by the fact that it uses only one cooking pot; it simply involves throwing all the ingredients, in any old order, into it.

As with the tagine, the *tangia* takes its name from the vessel in which it is cooked, a type of large eastern-style earthenware vase-shaped container with a rounded base and open neck, but without the handles. The top is covered with oiled greaseproof (waxed) paper, tied around the neck and pierced with two or three fine holes. Filled with its precious contents, the tangia is then carried to the local communal oven and left to cook in the glowing embers for several hours, often overnight. This dish can also be made at home in a large cooking pan set over a low heat or in a casserole with a tightly fitting lid placed in the oven set to a low temperature for at least six hours.

Dates sold loose are superior to those sold in boxes. They are sometimes steeped in honey, but are equally delicious eaten plain, provided that they are ripe and not over-dry.

The main ingredients of Moroccan nougat, known as jabane are crushed gum arabic, sugared egg white and toasted, whole almonds.

At the beginning of the summer season, newly picked almonds are eaten fresh, then a portion of the harvest is preserved for use in winter cooking. On the dried fruit stalls, figs are sold loose or threaded on string to form a chain.

Small pine nuts; the kernels sometimes feature in Moroccan patisserie.

Prunes are used to add flavour to lamb and chicken tagines. Those dried in the traditional way should be soaked beforehand in water for several hours.

الثمار الجافة DRIED FRUITS

Figs threaded on strings, raisins sold loose, glistening
dates, prunes, apricots and almonds, all create a palette of
ochre-brown hues, in the markets. Symbols of prosperity
and happiness, dried fruits are the fruits of choice to
celebrate the rites of birth, marriage and death. Served plain
or filled with almond paste, dates are offered to visitors as
a gesture of hospitality. The same applies in the south of
Morocco, where newlyweds are greeted with a shower of
dates. Apricot trees, fig trees and date palms flower at the
heart of the oases, and are irrigated by the water from deep
within the ground. In September and October, the markets
of the south are overflowing with all kinds of dates. Sweet,
firm, soft, plump, some varieties are sold dry, others made
into a paste, packed and sold by the piece. In February,
almond trees flower in their thousands in the southern Atlas
region. The brown skins of the almonds, used in tagines and
sweet dishes, are removed after blanching in boiling water for a
few seconds. Fig trees adapt to all types of soil and their fruit,
which is harvested in the summertime, is laid out to dry before
being preserved in large earthenware jars. Prunes or *mechmech*,
small aromatic apricots, are perfect for adding mild flavour
to lamb tagine.

These small-sized apricots, called mechmech *are
highly aromatic. They grow in oases, in the shade
of the date palms.*

Chicken k'dra with almonds and onions

This pigeon- (squab-) based recipe is served to newlyweds on the day following the wedding night. The main ingredients of the k'dra sauce are butter, finely chopped onions, parsley, pepper, salt and saffron.

SERVES 5
PREPARATION TIME: 15 MINUTES
COOKING TIME: 45 MINUTES

100 G (SCANT 1 CUP) ALMONDS
1 LARGE FREE-RANGE CHICKEN
SALT, PEPPER
LARGE PINCH OF SAFFRON
100 G (SCANT ½ CUP) BUTTER
750 G (1½ LB) ONIONS,
FINELY CHOPPED
HANDFUL OF PARSLEY

Blanch the almonds and remove the skins.

Cut the chicken into pieces. Put the pieces in a heavy pan with the giblets and season generously with salt and pepper. Add the saffron, butter, half the onion, the almonds and about 400 ml (1¾ cups) water. Cover and cook over medium heat for about 30 minutes. Turn the chicken pieces occasionally, adding more water, if required.

The chicken is cooked when the meat falls easily off the bone. Remove the chicken, set aside and keep hot.

Chop the parsley and add to the pan with the remaining onion and a pinch of salt. Mix well and cook for 10–15 minutes more, stirring occasionally.

When the onion mixture is cooked, return the chicken to the pan to heat the meat through.

Serve covered with the almonds and onions.

Prune tagine with almonds

Serves 8

Preparation time: 30 minutes

Cooking time: 1¼ hours (using a pressure cooker)

24 prunes

1.5 kg (3 lb) boned shoulder of lamb

1 teaspoon salt

5 tablespoons oil plus extra for roasting the almonds

1 teaspoon ground ginger

pinch of powdered saffron

2 onions, finely chopped

3 cloves garlic, finely chopped

4 tablespoons caster (superfine) sugar

125 g (1 cup) almonds

2 cinnamon sticks

1 tablespoon ground cinnamon

1 tablespoon clear honey

This sweet and savoury flavoured tagine, made with prunes and almonds, is an Andalusian culinary speciality that is reserved for festive occasions.

Place the prunes in a bowl, cover with water and leave to swell.

Cut the lamb into pieces.

Place the meat in a pressure cooker with the salt, oil, ginger, saffron, 1 onion and the garlic. Cover with water and stir. Close the lid firmly, bring to high pressure and cook for 20 minutes. Remove the pressure cooker from the heat to reduce the pressure, then remove the lid and continue cooking, uncovered, over low heat. When the meat is cooked through, add the second onion.

Stir in 1 tablespoon of sugar and cook for a further 15 minutes, turning the meat frequently. Remove the meat and set aside to keep hot. Reserve the sauce.

Meanwhile, blanch the almonds. Heat a little oil in a frying pan (skillet) and fry the almonds over high heat until golden brown, taking care they do not burn. Drain the almonds on kitchen paper (paper towels).

Drain the prunes and simmer in a pan containing the reserved sauce from the meat. When the prunes are almost cooked, add the remaining sugar, cinnamon sticks, ground cinnamon and honey. Simmer until the prunes have absorbed the sugar.

Place the meat and prunes in a tagine or suitable serving dish, drizzle with the sauce and sprinkle with the roasted almonds.

Almond-stuffed chicken with semolina and raisins

SERVES 4
PREPARATION TIME: 1 HOUR
COOKING TIME: 1 HOUR

FOR THE STUFFING
75 G (¾ CUP) ALMONDS
2 TABLESPOONS GROUNDNUT (PEANUT) OIL
100 G (3⅔ CUP) COUSCOUS GRAINS, STEAMED
100 G (¾ CUP) RAISINS
½ TEASPOON RAS-EL-HANOUT
SALT

1.5 KG (3 LB) CHICKEN
½ BUNCH OF PARSLEY, CHOPPED
1 LARGE ONION, THINLY SLICED
3 TABLESPOONS OIL
1 TABLESPOON BUTTER
1 TABLESPOON GROUND GINGER
PINCH OF SAFFRON
½ TABLESPOON SALT
1 TEASPOON GROUND PEPPER

For the stuffing: blanch the almonds and remove the skins. Heat the oil in a frying pan (skillet) and, when it is sizzling hot, fry the almonds, taking care they do not burn. Drain on kitchen paper (paper towels) and chop coarsely.

Mix all the stuffing ingredients together and stuff the chicken with the mixture.

Place the parsley and the onion in a large pan. Add the oil, butter and spices. Cover with 1 litre (4 cups) water, season with the salt and pepper, mix well and add the chicken. Bring to the boil. Turn the chicken over, reduce the heat and cook for about 30 minutes, turning the chicken 3–4 times. Preheat the oven to 220°C (425°F), Gas Mark 7. Place the chicken in a roasting tin (pan) and brown in the hot oven. In the meantime, reduce the sauce.

Serve in a tagine *slaoui*, a dish originally from Salé, a town near Rabat.

WINE الخمر

Over the past couple of decades, Moroccan wine producers have had to respond to increasingly discerning consumer expectations by overhauling production in the country's wine-growing regions, planting new vines, and investing in new technology production methods at their wineries. Although the Romans introduced the vine to Morocco in the second century AD, wine-making did not expand as an industry for another 15 centuries or so, when French agricultural workers developed viticulture in the Meknès and Oujda regions – in the east of the country – and in the Atlantic coastal area. Today, oak-aged wines are enhanced by the rich aromas derived from being aged in traditional oak barrels, but this painstaking and protracted procedure is reserved for top-of-the-range, quality wines such as the *Medallion* (reds and whites) and the *Beauvallon* label, produced by two local top wine-makers at the Meknès and Thalvin-Ebertec cellars. These wines are produced from a single, quality blend of grape varieties (merlot, chardonnay, cabernet sauvignon). The *Gris de Boulaouane* is renowned for its subtle aroma. This particularly pale-coloured rosé wine is produced from two grape types – cinsault and doukkali – both varieties that can withstand the extreme dryness of climate and terrain, and naturally yield black grapes with large seeds and white juice. This clear, light, slightly tannic wine requires only brief maceration. Equally rated among the most coveted wines to be produced in Morocco are the lively, fruity, dry white *Gris de Guerrouane* and a more recent addition, the *S de Siroua* that pairs marvellously with meat tagine dishes.

Calf's feet

SERVES 6
PREPARATION TIME: 30 MINUTES
COOKING TIME: 1¼ HOURS

1 LARGE ONION, THINLY SLICED
1 CLOVE GARLIC, CRUSHED
100 ML (SCANT ½ CUP) OLIVE OIL
1 TABLESPOON MILD CHILLI POWDER
2 CINNAMON STICKS
1 TABLESPOON GROUND GINGER
½ TEASPOON SAFFRON
½ BUNCH FLAT LEAF PARSLEY, CHOPPED
1 TEASPOON GROUND WHITE PEPPER
SALT
3 CALF'S FEET, HALVED LENGTHWAYS
250 G (1 CUP) CHICKPEAS (GARBANZO BEANS),
SOAKED OVERNIGHT AND DRAINED
100 G (½ CUP) WHEAT, SOAKED OVERNIGHT
AND DRAINED

Place the onion, garlic, olive oil, spices, parsley, pepper, salt in a large, heavy pan. Add water to cover and mix well.
Add the calf's feet and chickpeas (garbanzos). Stir all the ingredients again, thoroughly.
Bring to the boil. Turn the feet over and bring back to the boil.
Cover the pan, reduce the heat and simmer for about 1 hour. Keep a check and add extra hot water, if required.
When the calf's feet and chickpeas (garbanzos) are cooked and tender, add the wheat. Simmer on low heat for about 15 minutes; the sauce should be rich and thick, but not greasy.
For a variation on this recipe, use rice instead of wheat and add a handful of raisins.
The flavour of this dish benefits from preparing it the day before it is served.

Offal is a highly prized Moroccan delicacy and a vital ingredient in the preparation of special dishes for the feast of Aïd el Kébir, the festival of the sacrificial sheep.

Lambs' brains in chermoula

SERVES 4
PREPARATION TIME: 45 MINUTES
COOKING TIME: 15 MINUTES

2 LAMBS' BRAINS
1 TABLESPOON VINEGAR
4 TABLESPOONS OIL
2 CLOVES GARLIC
½ BUNCH OF CORIANDER (CILANTRO), CHOPPED
½ BUNCH OF PARSLEY, CHOPPED
1 TEASPOON MILD CHILLI POWDER
PINCH OF HOT CHILLI POWDER OR ¼ TEASPOON HARISSA
SALT
4 TABLESPOONS LEMON JUICE

Clean the lambs' brains in vinegar and water and remove the membranes. Rinse and cut the brains into pieces. Heat the oil in a large, heavy pan; add the pieces of brains, garlic, coriander (cilantro), parsley and spices. Simmer for 15 minutes or until the sauce is thickened, stirring occasionally.
Serve hot or cold. Sprinkle the mixture with the lemon juice just before serving.

Liver in m'chermel sauce

SERVES 8
PREPARATION TIME: 30 MINUTES
COOKING TIME: 30 MINUTES

1 KG (2 LB) CALF'S LIVER
5 TABLESPOONS OIL
500 ML (GENEROUS 2 CUPS) WATER
½ TEASPOON SALT
4 CLOVES GARLIC, FINELY CHOPPED
1 BUNCH OF PARSLEY, FINELY CHOPPED
1 TABLESPOON CHILLI POWDER
2 TABLESPOONS VINEGAR
DICED RIND OF 1 PRESERVED LEMON

Cut the liver into large pieces and cook in the oil. Leave to cool, then cut into smaller pieces.
In a heavy pan, bring the water, salt, garlic, parsley, chilli powder, and the liver to the boil. Lower the heat, add the vinegar and slowly reduce the sauce, but do not let it get too thick.
Serve cold, garnished with the preserved lemon rind.

Makfoul

Serves 8
Preparation time: 15 minutes
Cooking time: 1¼ hours

150 ml (⅔ cup) oil
1.5 kg (3 lb) mutton or lamb, diced
3 cinnamon sticks
1 tablespoon ground cinnamon
generous pinch of saffron
1 teaspoon powdered chilli powder
1 teaspoon ground ginger
1 teaspoon ground pepper
2 kg (4 lb) onions
4 large ripe tomatoes
caster (superfine) sugar
salt

Heat the oil in a large, heavy pan and lightly brown the meat, with the cinnamon sticks, a little salt and half the spices. Add about 400 ml (1¾ cups) water.

In a bowl, combine the remaining spices, a little salt and sufficient water to make a thin paste.

Cut the onions in half, but if they are very large, cut into three. Halve the tomatoes. Dip the onions into the bowl containing the spice paste; then position the coated onions on top of the meat, cut surface downwards, entirely covering the meat. Arrange the tomato halves on top, cut side upwards. Cover the pan and cook for about 1 hour over medium heat without stirring, but keep a regular check to make sure that it is not sticking and add hot water if necessary.

Arrange the meat and vegetables in a tagine in the same order as in the pan (meat on the bottom, onions and tomatoes on top). Reserve the sauce. This is a tricky procedure that requires a slotted spoon (skimmer).

Preheat the oven to 200°C (400°F), Gas Mark 6.

Spread the sauce over the contents of the tagine. Any excess sauce can be kept warm and used for basting during the final cooking. Sprinkle with a little sugar and cook in the oven for the final 30–45 minutes.

When the onions are well-cooked and golden brown, remove the tagine from the oven. Carefully skim off the sauce, add to any remaining sauce and reduce over high heat for a few minutes, until the sauce is of thick and smooth.

Pour the sauce over the dish and serve hot.

COOKING EQUIPMENT

لوازم الطبخ

Often huge and sparsely furnished, a traditional Moroccan kitchen usually has only rustic-style cooking equipment, the bare essentials for preparing a wide variety of dishes. Essential pots and pans include the *qadra*, a large copper cooking pot, a cast-iron or stainless steel container, used for cooking large quantities of vegetables and meat. Couscous is prepared in a *gsââ*, a large round shallow, earthenware or wooden dish, and cooked in a couscoussier, consisting of two separate sections. The meat and vegetables are cooked in the stainless steel or tin-plate bottom section, while the couscous grains swell up in the sieve-like steamer basket, placed directly above the contents in the lower section. A slotted spoon (skimmer) is used to separate the vegetables and meat from the bouillon, and a ladle to moisten the couscous. Tagine *slaoui*, durable round earthenware dishes with pointed lids, are essential for both cooking and keeping all sorts of different dishes hot. Tagines are slotted into hollow copper dishes that protect table surfaces from the hot food. A pestle and mortar makes easy work of grinding spices and crushing herbs and garlic. Various metal moulds are used for preparing pastry. The most important piece of equipment, however, is the water boiler, which is always full of water and on stand-by for making tea. The *tbika*, an esparto grass wicker basket with a pointed cover, protects bread from getting dusty. Before the advent of gas cookers, a round earthenware *kanoun* was the main cooking appliance available in the kitchens of Morocco.

ROSE PERFUMES

عطير الزهور

According to the legend and to lyrical poetic outpourings, *Rosa damascena*, the rose of Damascus, was introduced to Morocco by Berber pilgrims returning from Mecca, who were overwhelmed by the scent of this flower. Thereafter, wild roses have grown in tightly packed hedges, oblivious to the cold dry climate, in the foothills of the ochre-coloured High Atlas Mountains.

In springtime each year, thousands of fresh roses are gathered and sold in markets or delivered to the two distillation factories in the Kelaa M'Gouna region. Transformed into rosewater or rose essence, these flowers are the very symbol of Moroccan hospitality. During festivals or at elegant dinner parties, rose petals are strewn on tables; it is also customary to sprinkle newlyweds with rosewater contained in *mrachas*, small squat-shaped, glass perfume bottles with long silver plated necks. Aromatic qualities aside, rosewater is also used in certain pastries such as the coiled serpent-shaped *m'henchas*. The rose-based liquid extract used in pomades or in syrup mixtures is said to cure infections. Rosewater is also a component in a whole panoply of Moroccan beauty products, such as henna and kohl. As a compress for tired eyes or mixed with henna as a hair colourant, rose petals offer surprising cosmetic benefits.

In May, every year, the Kelaa M'Gouna rose festival celebrates the end of the rose harvest. Young girls decked out in lavish dresses, wearing crowns made of roses, and adorned with necklaces of fresh flowers, shower passers-by with a profusion of rose petals.

Morocco produces around three tonnes of rose essence annually, of which approximately a third is exported to French perfume manufacturers. Five kilos (10 lb) of fresh roses are required to produce 1 kilo (2 lb) of dried rose buds.

In Muslim society, the rose is the queen of flowers, and often the subject of Arab poetry. It was the renowned tenth-century philosopher and mathematician, Avicenne, who first discovered the distillation process.

Pastilla with milk

SERVES 8
PREPARATION TIME: 30 MINUTES
COOKING TIME: 5 MINUTES PER SHEET

200 G (1¾ CUPS) ALMONDS
200 G (1 CUP) CASTER (SUPERFINE) SUGAR
200 ML (SCANT 1 CUP) OIL
8 SHEETS FILO PASTRY (OR 16 SHEETS BRIK)
750 ML (3 CUPS) MILK
1 TABLESPOON ORANGE-FLOWER WATER

Blanch the almonds in boiling water for 5 minutes. Remove the skins and dry the almonds thoroughly. Heat half the oil in a frying pan (skillet). When the oil is sizzling hot, fry the almonds until they are a light golden brown, taking care they do not burn.

Remove immediately, drain off excess oil on kitchen paper (paper towels) and coarsely grind the almonds in a food processor together with half of the sugar.

Cut 16 rounds, 20-cm/8-inch diameter, from the filo sheets and keep covered with a damp cloth to prevent them from drying out.

Heat the remaining oil in a large frying pan (skillet) and when it is sizzling hot, brown the filo rounds, one at a time. Stack the fried rounds, as you go along, on a wire rack, inserting a piece of kitchen paper (paper towel) between each one.

Place the first round on a large serving dish and dust with the almonds. Place the next round on top and dust with the almonds. Continue to build up a stack, alternating each pastry round with a sprinkling of almonds. This stage of the recipe can be prepared well in advance.

Just before serving, boil the milk with the orange-flower water and the remaining sugar.

Gently remove the kitchen paper (paper towels) and carefully pour the milk over and around the stack. Serve immediately.

Lukewarm cream can be used instead of milk flavoured with orange-flower water to moisten pastilla, which should be served immediately.

HONEY

Honey has always played an important part in ancient culinary practice. It was made sacred by Islam in this verse from the Quran: 'From the entrails of bees comes forth a many-coloured liquid which heals mankind.' (XVI, 68). Honey from acacia, clover or alfalfa, honey from heather or lavender, thyme or thuja, eucalyptus honey, honey from fine herbs or wild bay from the Rif region; honey is a staple ingredient of the Berber diet, as an accompaniment for bread and mint tea. Throughout the month of Ramadan, it envelops *chebbakiyas*, twists of fried pastry, dredged with sesame seeds, which are served at the same time as *harira*, at the precise moment when the fast comes to an end. Honey is used as a topping for pancakes — *beghrir, briouats* with almonds, or *baklaouas*. It is used to flavour sweetened couscous and spicy tagines where its quality is essential for the flavour and consistency of the sauce. Honey features in the preparation of caramelized onions, spiced with ras-el-hanout, flavoured with olive oil and served with fried fish. It accompanies semolina on the day of the festival celebrating the birth of the prophet Mouloud. In the Atlas regions, a young bride rubs her fingers with honey before making her first couscous dish, in order to attract a gentle way of life and harmony, in her new role as a married woman.

DESSERTS الحلوي

Small cakes for all occasions, home-baked pastries are always popular at any time of day. The mistress of the house always makes sure that she is has a good supply to accompany mint tea. Small cakes, lined up on large plates, play an integral role on festive occasions. Large cakes, on the other hand, do not feature in Morocco's cake-making tradition. Fried in oil or baked in the oven, small cakes ooze with honey or almond paste filling; honey is also found in *ghoribas* with almonds, *rghaifs*, *m'henchas*, shaped like coiled serpents, *briouats, makrouts, fekkas*...

Dates with honey

SERVES 8
PREPARATION TIME: 15 MINUTES

500 G (GENEROUS 3 CUPS) DATES, PITTED
2 TABLESPOONS HONEY
2 TABLESPOONS GROUND CINNAMON
1 TABLESPOON SEMOLINA
PINCH OF GROUND GUM ARABIC
PINCH OF FRESHLY GRATED NUTMEG
1 TEASPOON ORANGE-FLOWER WATER

Dice the dates. Place all the ingredients in an earthenware bowl and mix by hand until the mixture forms a paste.

This confection is served at breakfast and also at other times according to preference, accompanied by bread and thin curls of butter.

ABOVE
A serpent curled around itself, almond m'hencha, *made with sheets of brik pastry, is not a simple cake to prepare.*

Bite-size cinnamon biscuits (cookies)

MAKES 50
PREPARATION TIME: 30 MINUTES
COOKING TIME: 30 MINUTES

250 G (2 CUPS) PLAIN (ALL-PURPOSE) FLOUR
1 SACHET (ENVELOPE) DRIED YEAST
125 G (GENEROUS ½ CUP) CASTER (SUPERFINE) SUGAR
½ TEASPOON GROUND CINNAMON
80 G (¾ CUP) GROUND ALMONDS
150 G (⅔ CUP) BUTTER, MELTED
ICING (CONFECTIONERS') SUGAR FOR DREDGING

Preheat the oven to 150°C (300°F), Gas Mark 2.

Sift the flour into a bowl. Mix in the yeast, caster (superfine) sugar, cinnamon and ground almonds.

Make a well in the centre. Pour in the butter and bring all together lightly by hand to form a ball. Divide the dough into small balls by rolling on a flat surface with the palm. Lightly flatten them with a fork. Place on a greased baking (cookie) sheet, 2.5 cm (1 inch) apart. Set aside for 10 minutes.

Bake for 30 minutes. Remove from the oven and dredge with icing (confectioners') sugar.

DATES الثمر

In the depths of the palm groves of southern Morocco, a rather unusual activity announces the start of the date-picking season. Agile men climb, barefoot, to the very top of the palm trees, balancing on the 'steps' created up the length of the trunks by the stumps of cut down palm branches. The sounds of machete blows resound from tree to tree. Once the dates have been chopped down on to large sheets spread out on the ground below, the next stage involves the women – sorting and grading the heavy orangey-coloured bunches of dates.

The date palm is not naturally self-pollinating: neither wind nor insects alone can adequately pollinate it. Consequently, man has to resort to a form of artificial insemination. At the beginning of spring, a specialist gathers the spathes, the long white flowers that grow at the centre of the tree and contain the pollen grains, from the male palm trees. He dissects the spathes, blade by blade, and then slides them into the half-open spathes of the female tree, which he then ties in place with a palm frond. Once pollination has been successfully accomplished, the knot is broken. Five months later, towards the end of summer when the dates are fully ripe, the harvest may begin. A mature palm tree produces up to fifty kilos (110 lb) of dates.

Makrouts

MAKES 50
PREPARATION TIME: 1 HOUR
STANDING TIME: 4 HOURS
COOKING TIME: 30 MINUTES

FOR THE FILLING:
1 KG (SCANT 6½ CUPS) CHOPPED DATES, PITTED
2 TABLESPOONS BUTTER, MELTED
1 TEASPOON CASTER (SUPERFINE) SUGAR
1 TEASPOON GROUND CINNAMON
PINCH OF GROUND CLOVES

FOR THE DOUGH:
500 G (2⅔ CUPS) FINE GRAIN SEMOLINA
250 G (1⅓ CUPS) MEDIUM GRAIN SEMOLINA
4 TABLESPOONS CASTER (SUPERFINE) SUGAR
PINCH OF DRIED YEAST
250 G (1 CUP) BUTTER, MELTED
PINCH OF SALT
200 ML (SCANT 1 CUP) ORANGE-FLOWER WATER PLUS
A DASH FOR COATING
500 ML (GENEROUS 2 CUPS) COLD WATER
1 LITRE (4 CUPS) OIL FOR FRYING
500 G (2 CUPS) HONEY
PINCH OF GROUND GUM ARABIC

For the dough: put the semolinas in a bowl and mix in the sugar, yeast, butter and salt. Gradually fold in the orange-flower water and sufficient cold water to form a dough. Cover and let stand for 4 hours in a warm place.

For the filling: mix together the dates, butter, sugar and spices into a paste. Roll the filling into little batons about 2 cm (¾ inch) thick and 20 cm (8 inches) long. Set aside to chill.

Make 20-cm (8-inches) long 'sausages' from the dough and, with a finger, make an indentation down the middle and insert a baton of filling. Neatly seal the dough edges over the filling and cut the filled 'sausages' into 5-cm (2-inches) pieces, using a pastry cutter. Heat the oil in a frying pan (skillet) and when it is sizzling hot, brown the makrouts for a few minutes, then drain on kitchen paper (paper towels). Blend together the honey, a dash of orange-flower water and the gum arabic in a separate bowl. Dip the makrouts, one at a time to coat. Leave to cool before serving.

Kaak
(ring-shaped loaf with sesame seeds)

SERVES 8-10
PREPARATION TIME: 30 MINUTES
STANDING TIME: 3 HOURS
COOKING TIME: 30 MINUTES

1 KG (8 CUPS) PLAIN (ALL-PURPOSE) FLOUR
150 G (⅔ CUP) BUTTER
2 BEATEN EGGS
500 ML (GENEROUS 2 CUPS) MILK
250 G (GENEROUS 1 CUP) CASTER
(SUPERFINE) SUGAR
25 G (1 OZ) FRESH YEAST, (PREPARED
BEFOREHAND IN A LITTLE WARM WATER AND
LEFT TO RISE FOR 10–15 MINUTES)
1 SACHET (ENVELOPE) DRIED YEAST
PINCH OF SALT
1 TABLESPOON GROUND SESAME SEEDS
1 TABLESPOON GROUND FENNEL SEEDS
PINCH OF GROUND GUM ARABIC
1 TABLESPOON SESAME SEEDS, TO DECORATE

Combine all the ingredients into a firm, but smooth dough. Form into pairs of 15-cm (6-inch) long strips. Intertwine each pair of strips to create a 'bracelet' effect, sealing the ends firmly into a ring. Place the rings on a greased baking (cookie) sheet, cover with cloth and leave to rise in a warm place for about 3 hours.

Preheat the oven to 220°C (425°F), Gas Mark 7.

Sprinkle the rings with sesame seeds and bake for 30 minutes, but keep a check to make sure that they are not burning.

The small hard dates found in Marrakech are chopped and made into filling for makrouts, as well as fillings for other types of confectionery.

Fresh dates are also stuffed with almond or walnut paste.

In the desert regions, where hospitality is legendary, tea is served strong, very sweet, and often without mint. It is customary to accept three glasses of tea, in close succession. In the vast open expanses of the South Sahara, marabouts, small white buildings, break the monotony of the horizon. They protect the tombs of holy men, the subjects of true worship. The nomad's companion, the dromedary, is renowned for its steadfast demeanour. It can go without water for a whole week. Then, to rehydrate, it requires 100 litres (26 gallons) of water. The dromedary makes do with prickly plants that grow at ground level and which burst into multicoloured flowers after a single downpour.

Editors

Odile Perrard and Valérie Tognali

Graphic Design

Sabine Houplain

Production

Frédérique de Redon

Translation of Arabic titles

Fella Saïdi-Tournoux

First published by Editions du Chêne, an imprint of Hachette-Livre
43 Quai de Grenelle, Paris 75905, Cedex 15, France
Under the title Saveurs Marocaines
© 2001, Editions du Chêne, Hachette-Livre
All rights reserved

English language translation produced by Translate-a-Book, Oxford

This edition published by Hachette Illustrated UK,
Octopus Publishing Group Ltd,
2–4 Heron Quays, London, E14 4JP
© 2004, English translation, Octopus Publishing Group Ltd, London
ISBN-13 : 978-1-84430-107-2
ISBN : 1-84430-107-9
Printed in Singapore by Tien Wah Press